I0476678

Behind The Click

How Builders and Remodelers
Can Leverage Their Own Online
Media To Attract Highly-Qualified
Leads and Sell More Homes and
Remodels

© Copyright 2016 by Inbound Mill, Inc - All Rights Reserved.

This document is geared towards providing exact and reliable information in regards to the topic and issue covered. The publication is sold with the idea that the publisher is not required to render, officially permitted, or otherwise, qualified services. If advice is necessary, legal or professional, a practiced individual in the profession should be ordered.

From a Declaration of Principles which was accepted and approved equally by a Committee of the American Bar Association and a Committee of Publishers and Associations.

In no way is it legal to reproduce, duplicate, or transmit any part of this document in either electronic means or in printed format. Recording of this publication is strictly prohibited and any storage of this document is not allowed unless with written permission from the publisher. All Rights Reserved.

The information provided herein is stated to be truthful and consistent, in that any liability, in terms of inattention or otherwise, by any usage or abuse of any policies, processes, or directions contained within is the solitary and utter responsibility of the recipient reader. Under no circumstances will any legal responsibility or blame be held against the

stretch, but I'm just glad that I'm both a theorist and an entrepreneur who is willing to push the envelope of what it means to be "human".

It is sensible to take turns doing demanding jobs, whether with people or with geese flying south.

Geese honk from behind to encourage those up front to keep up their speed.

What message do we give when we honk from behind?

Finally - and this is important - when a goose gets sick or is wounded by gunshot, and falls out of the formation, two other geese fall out with that goose and follow it down to lend help and protection. They stay with the fallen goose until it is able to fly or until it dies; and only then do they launch out on their own, or with another formation to catch up with their own group.

This phenomenon explains why I seek to understand the subtle intersection of technology and society's behavioral patterns. We show up as "human" on these online platforms, yet they all paint a different picture about us within the confines of their "rules". CEOs from publicly traded companies are now forced to pay attention to that one customer on Twitter because the platform gives her an easy outlet to express her opinions about them. Is society getting closer to moving in one direction through the enablement of technology? Perhaps that's a bit of a

Preface

Next Autumn, when you see geese heading south for the winter, flying in a "V" formation, you might consider what science has discovered as to why they fly that way. As each bird flaps its wings, it creates an uplift for the bird immediately following. By flying in a "V" formation, the whole flock adds at least 71 percent greater flying range than if each bird flew on its own.

People who share a common direction and sense of community can get where they are going more quickly and easily, because they are travelling on the thrust of one another.

When a goose falls out of formation, it suddenly feels the drag and resistance of trying to go it alone and quickly gets back into formation to take advantage of the lifting power of the bird in front.

If we have the sense of a goose, we will stay in formation with those people who are heading the same way we are.

When the head goose gets tired, it rotates back in the wing and another goose flies point.

TO CHRISTINA

For your love

publisher for any reparation, damages, or monetary loss due to the information herein, either directly or indirectly.

Respectful authors own all copyrights not held by the publisher.

The information herein is offered for informational purposes solely. The presentation of the information is without contract or any type of guarantee assurance.

The trademarks that are used without any consent, and the publication of the trademark is without permission or backing by the trademark owner. All trademarks and brands within this book are for clarifying purposes only and are the owned by the owners themselves, not affiliated with this document.

This book was written, edited, and published in a reasonable amount of time. *Well, a reasonable amount of time, 14 years of mistakes, and a small army of really dedicated team members and wonderful clients and customers.* I'm so grateful for the support and patience you've given me.

How To Use This Book

This book was written to be both practical and informative, so that you could pick up the book as you would an instructional manual and flip to the right page to understand how to get the results for exactly what you need.

All of the chapters in the book were derived from the most frequently asked questions that I've gotten from consulting with clients on their marketing and sales systems.

While there are many questions that get asked over and over again, only a small handful of people know enough about digital marketing to ask me the questions we both know they *should* be asking.

So that's what I've done- I've compiled a book of answers to my most frequently asked questions in addition to giving answers to the *should ask* questions when it comes to procuring more qualified leads and clients online.

I started my agency to help others in the built environment who are willing to invest in a partnership to automate their marketing and sales systems.

I intend for you to glean some of the insights that have helped us generate awesome results for our clients. I hope that the contents in this book will deliver the context you were looking for as well as the tools to enable you to make the right choices in your business.

You can also contact me anytime at bobby@inboundmill.com.

Table Of Contents

Introduction...19

CHAPTER 1
The Novelty of Paying for Digital Assets...................................27

CHAPTER 2
The Scorecard of Important Numbers 33

CHAPTER 3
The Zero Moment of Truth...45

CHAPTER 4
Pay Per Click Vs. Getting Free Clicks 51

CHAPTER 5
The Napkin $5,000 Quarterly Marketing Plan 61

CHAPTER 6
The Most Important Web Tools You'll Need.............................71

CHAPTER 7
2 Questions: How Long and How Much? 83

CHAPTER 8
Differentiation Produces Quality Clients..................................93

CHAPTER 9
How Many Consultations Does It Take?................................101

CHAPTER 10
Cracking The First Page of Google 111

CHAPTER 11
Social Media Sounds Like A Waste of Media 127

CHAPTER 12
The Power In Broadcasting Your Company's Diary...............139

CHAPTER 13
Inbound Marketing Is The New Marketing............................149

CHAPTER 14
Getting Those Form Fields Filled To The Brim 161

CHAPTER 15
How To Create Content With ROI In Mind............................169

CHAPTER 16
The Intersection of Consistent Leads and Marketing
Automation 175

CHAPTER 17
Leads Are Great, But Qualified Leads Are Even Better.........187

CHAPTER 18
Case Studies: A Closer Look...197

Conclusion...213

Introduction

Greatness is a spiritual condition worthy to excite love, interest, and admiration; and the outward proof of possessing greatness is that we excite love, interest, and admiration.

-Matthew Arnold

I wrote this book for all of the builders, remodelers, and businesses in the built environment looking to gain a competitive edge in today's markets and all the diligent and focused business owners who either have a weekly scorecard of their most important numbers that move the needle for their businesses or really want to implement a system to help them keep score.

"It's not your fault, Friend".

If the "*business* guru" were a talking plush toy with a pre-recorded list of phrases, then this one would surely crack the list.

And it's true.

To an extent.

You can hardly be faulted for trying new online solutions like Angie's List or Houzz as the foundation for growing into new marketing channels online when nearly every sleazy marketer to spring out of the bushes puts some new spin on it.

But what's staggering is how single family home dwellers have made such a convincing argument for you to be online.

Buyer behavior today has changed.

"By 2020, customers will manage 85% of their relationships without ever talking to a human."

Stats like that are what cause us to move away from the status quo, to stop relying on our past referrals that aren't allowing us to grow our revenues, and search for someplace online where we can park our digital signage, so to speak.

To the extent that when we FAIL to reach our market with our message, instead of pointing a finger at the broken system, **we turn a judging eye at the platform that didn't produce results!**

You see, it's not that these platforms don't work. They do.

We just need a methodology and a strategy that leverages the right platforms to get the results we're looking for.

This book is about leverage.

It contains the methodology that allows my agency to deliver consistent results in the form of qualified leads and clients.

Traditional advertising and sales is going to die and if you don't adopt this new methodology, you will be left in the dust.

I'm going to show you something that will change the way you get clients forever, plus make it easier and way more sustainable.

Here it is in a nutshell:

You help your future clients with remarkable content.

All homeowners and homebuyers still have problems and needs. They don't want to hear about your product. They want to hear how to solve their problems.

This is called **Inbound Marketing** and the time to start using it is NOW.

Inbound Marketing is all about ATTRACTING your audience to you instead of pushing your product on them.

Inbound Marketing is all about creating content that will help your target client – Answering their questions, solving their problems, and starting a relationship.

Once the relationship starts, they will begin to trust you as an authority and be curious about what solutions you have that can solve their problems.

Then you have 5000x the power.

They like you, they know you, they trust you, and then they buy from you.

Here's the Hocus-Pocus Unicorn Dust Part

So this is the part where I would say it's all about 'quality content' and you would throw your hands up in the air and laugh at my face.

Well, let me show you how we use inbound / content marketing to actually put dollars in the bank.

It's insanely simple:

- You identify problems that your target client has.

- You write articles about them.

- You publish them on your blog.

- You promote those posts though your email list, Facebook, Twitter, etc.

- Your clients find them, read them, then see your firm as an authority.

- They get curious about your solutions.

- They subscribe to your list or download an ebook offer after reading a post.

- You send them more awesome answers to their questions with an opportunity to contact you.

- They book & hop on a call with one of your sales counselors.

- Sales counselors have the easiest sell in the world because the lead already knows, likes and trusts the company.

If you follow the advice laid out in this book, you can expect to lower your cost to acquire a client, have online assets that return dividends in the form of long term leads and clients, and scale your business to the level you've always dreamed about.

Let's begin.

CHAPTER 1
The Novelty of Paying for Digital Assets

Don't let the fear of losing be greater than the excitement of winning.

-Robert Kiyosaki

Yes, digital marketing can look like misty air. But only when you don't know what you're looking at or measuring. Let me explain.

It's not like you are building a home and you're able to see the actual home being built. That's tangible. I get that, but what we have to understand is that we are increasingly living in a data-driven world and your business is a part of this world, whether you like it or not.

Big data is the biggest buzz word out there and its tangibility has worth. High worth. Have you ever seen Moneyball? The movie is predicated on the premise that Baseball championships can be won by gathering insights from stats and leveraging that data to win games.

In the digital realm, everything is being tracked and recorded as data. It is a special time for marketers and advances in technology are making it incredibly easy for businesses to get valuable information in their markets. These days, you can track anything from a click to the location where you made that click. Conversations are recorded through many forms of communication; e-mails, phone records and social media posts can be kept and recorded. Google is one of the three largest e-mail services in the world and all e-mails sent and received are analyzed for market research.

All activities are tracked in the digital world. Internet browser logs keep a history and websites can see how we navigated their site; they can measure our purchase history and what we like or share. Sensors are everywhere collecting data in our phones where they can see what phone apps we use the most that are providing information about our hobbies and interests. Sensors collect ocean temperature and currents. Car insurance companies such as Progressive have sensors called Snapshot that monitors your driving patterns to see if you qualify for insurance premium discounts. New technology like smart watches or pedometers like the Fitbit can see how many steps you take per day, track your calorie intake or even monitor how well you slept during the night.

Almost every aspect of our lives is affected by data or analytics. From a business standpoint, analytics can be used to predict and improve business performance. With all this information floating around, it's very easy to see why analytics should not be overlooked. If you're not living in a data-driven world then quite simply, you're living under a rock.

The true value that my marketing agency is able to offer to my clientele is not in the tactics and activities that we perform to get results. It's not in the services that we provide, but rather the strategy that we're able to plan out based on the insights that we can gather from the data that we collect. When we produce monthly reporting, we look at data that we have collected and monitor key metrics that show whether or not our activities are producing a return for a business. There are about 5-7 main metrics or key performance indicators that indicate the health of your marketing. From those key performance indicators, you should be able to identify the necessary actions that must be taken to improve upon that metric. From those actions you'll be able to identify what impact they'll have on the bottom line of your company.

So the important lesson here is that data is everywhere and it can be utilized. It can inform your decisions and give you insights to take better actions to improve and accel your results. Do yourself a huge favor and keep an eye on the right KPIs. Your heartbeat is a KPI. It tells you whether or not you're alive. Do you have a heartbeat? If so, you know how to track a KPI.

Would you like to access our fast-start marketing bundle for builders and remodelers?

You'll get instant access to cheat sheets and guides that will fast-track you towards running your own marketing engine. Plus receive updates on my best marketing advice and a complimentary consultation offer where we'll map out the exact strategy to help you reach your goals.

Visit www.inboundmill.com/book-bundle

or text your first name and email address to (424) 652-6242

CHAPTER 2
The Scorecard of Important Numbers

Without big data analytics, companies are blind and deaf, wandering out onto the Web like deer on a freeway.

-Geoffrey Moore

It is estimated that more than 94% of homeowners and homebuyers start their search online.

So it makes sense that the health of your business directly ties to how people find, engage and interact with your company online. For many builders, current online marketing efforts might include a website, a Facebook page, a Twitter account and/ or a Houzz profile page. Although these are useful tools, many builders find it challenging to create a measurable connection between posts, pins, tweets, appointments, sales and closings.

Instead of measuring success by likes, repins and retweets and getting bogged down in data puke, you should focus on a few key metrics or as I like to call them: KPI's or Key Performance Indicators. These few key metrics will help you determine exactly how well your online marketing is working to create measurable returns for your business. These key metrics work as a compass, guiding you toward your annual sales goals and alerting you if your current marketing takes you off course.

My client William started off with very little to nothing. His social media following and website visits were next near to zero, so we decided to focus on a few key metrics in the beginning in order to guide his compass towards developing traction as a small volume homebuilder. The two metrics that we identified as important KPI's were his visit to lead conversation rate and the number of website visits he was receiving. These two KPI's were enough to work with to measure and improve. They were focused on driving eyeballs to his business.

Now your situation may be different. You may have accumulated more website visitors than my client did over the same period of time, and your focus might be to improve upon your lead to appointment conversion rate and also the overall size of your active lead list.

I'm going to introduce the core metrics that every builder should be keeping an eye on, especially if you're a low volume builder producing anywhere from $5 and $50 million a year in volume.

Website Traffic

Starting with website traffic, you must use a tracking program like Google Analytics, tally your total website traffic from the last 12 months, and divide this number by 12. This will be your average monthly traffic. By using a 12 month average, you can account for seasonal highs and lows. If you don't currently have Google Analytics or don't have access from your marketing partner or web developer, make getting access a priority.

As an owner of your company, you should be able to access and understand your website analytics even if you don't manage your own marketing.

A word of caution: Be careful not to misconstrue your website visits for quality visits because chances are that a lot of those visits might be spam. This was the case for one builder when he told me that he had around 650 visits per month. By the time I accessed his Google Analytics we identified that around 550 of those visits were coming from spam! In essence, he was really at ground zero and needed a lot of work done to drive more quality traffic to his website.

There is no right or wrong answer to this number. It's simply your starting point and we all have a starting point.

Visit To Lead Conversion Rate

The next metric to keep an eye on is your visit to lead conversion rate.

For the last 12 months, how many total unique leads were registered through your website? Divide that number by the total number of unique visitors to your website over the last 12 months. For example if you've received 200 online leads in the last year and had 10,000 unique website visitors, your conversion rate would be 2% which is roughly 22 divided by 10,000 unique website visitors.

Visitor to lead conversion is a cornerstone concept for builders. If you currently don't have a way of measuring this, make it a priority to add this tracking through your Google Analytics, your customer relationship management tool, your email service provider or any other tracking tool you use. More importantly, if you are a little bit more comfortable with Google Analytics, be sure to set up goal tracking inside Google Analytics where every lead that comes in through your website will be tracked and you will know how you measure up to this conversation rate.

Total Leads

A third metric is the overall size of your active lead list. This can be the number of people that you currently have on your list who haven't bought from you, who you're currently talking to, as well as prospects that you probably marked as a dead lead.

How many people do you email every month that are currently in your lead list? Active leads are leads that have opened at least one email in the last three months. If you have not emailed your list in more than three months, then be sure to do that. Determine what percentage of your lead list is still engaged by open rates and click through rates. Check to see who has clicked through and opened up your email. If you haven't emailed your list in a while it may take two or three emails over the course of a month to re-engage the people who previously opted in to your list.

Whenever our agency onboards a new client, we take a look at their active lead list, especially if they are starting with very little traffic on their website. We then take their active lead list and immediately send an email campaign to this list to reactivate the list just to find out who is still raising their hands to be marketed to. You will be surprised to find out just how many people in your list are going to re-engage.

It's always a good surprise and you might even end up re-activating some of your old clients.

Lead To Appointment Conversion Rate

Another metric is your lead to appointment conversion rate.

While it's a nice idea that everyone who registers on your website will immediately schedule an on-site appointment, write a contract and then close, I'm sure you also very well understand that online homeowners and homebuyers register on your website at all stages of their buying journey.

You should try to make it a point not to just focus on the low hanging fruit of buyers who are ready to buy today. Build your email list as a primary marketing asset that continually pays dividends, new appointments and sales now, and in the future.

Instead of tracking only how many new leads close to contract, measure the percentage of the total lead list that is converting to on-site appointments.

To measure your current lead to appointment conversion rate, add up all of your on-site appointments that came from an online lead and divide that by your total lead list. For example, if you have a list of a thousand leads and you schedule 10 appointments on average from that list per month, you have a list to appointment conversation rate of 1% which is 10 divided by 1,000. If you're not currently tracking this information or if your lead to appointment conversation rate is 0, don't let that discourage you. Just set-up a simple method for tracking this information going forward.

Appointment To Sales Conversion Rate

The next metric is your appointment to sales conversion rate.

Out of all the appointments that you schedule, what percentage of this converted to contract? If you have 10 appointments from your list and 5 convert to contract, then you have an appointment to sales conversion rate of 50%, which is about 5 out of 10. In most cases, this should be a 12 month average. However, if there has been a significant change in your market recently, up or down, a six month average may be more appropriate.

Sales To Closing Conversion Rate

Now let's talk about your sales to closing conversion, or simply, what's your cancellation rate?

Cancellations can occur for a variety of reasons including financing, job loss, competition, an existing home not selling, and cold feet, among others. If you write 5 sales contracts and 3 close, you have a sales to close ratio of 60%.

Monthly Average Referrals

We've all heard of monthly average referrals, the lost stage of the sales funnel. Tracking your referrals from existing homeowners and homebuyers is an effective component of an effective marketing plan for small and medium sized builders.

If you have closed 2500 homes and you received 25 homebuyer referrals, you have a referral rate of 1%. Your referral rate refers to on-site appointments with prospects that were directly referred from an existing homebuyer.

So once you've identified these core few metrics, you can visualize how well your online sales funnel is performing. You can start with a few metrics just as my client did with the first two metrics, where he just measured his website traffic and his visit to lead conversion rate.

Depending on where you are in your online marketing, you can adjust as you go.

Would you like to access our fast-start marketing bundle for builders and remodelers?

You'll get instant access to cheat sheets and guides that will fast-track you towards running your own marketing engine. Plus receive updates on my best marketing advice and a complimentary consultation offer where we'll map out the exact strategy to help you reach your goals.

Visit www.inboundmill.com/book-bundle

or text your first name and email address to (424) 652-6242

CHAPTER 3
The Zero Moment of Truth

"But there's one critical difference between old-fashioned word of mouth and the digital version. "Talking over the hedge is one-to-one," says Prof. Dave Reibstein, the William Stewart Woodside Professor at The Wharton School. "Digital word of mouth is one-to-millions. If you have a good experience, it's shared and re-shared with millions. You post it and suddenly, it's flying."

-Jim Lecinsky

Times have changed.

Imagine that you need a new entertainment system. You're in your family room, you reach for that old remote, and you just realized that you are better off with a state of the art flat screen tv and speaker system. You remember seeing a really cool ad for one in particular, but you'd rather read some reviews and product information before you head out to make that purchase. Your time is limited and making efficient use of your time is mandatory. Then after reading about 3 different articles comparing different products, you eventually make the trip to Best Buy to make your purchase, right?

This is the behavior of the modern consumer: multi-screen research. It's no longer a luxury but rather a necessary companion for assisting a purchase. People these days have access to such a wealth of information. Everything is only a click away and they seek information needed to make a more informed decision even after they have experienced the initial stimulus which is your advertisement.

A lot of builders are still relying on traditional broadcast methods to advertise their services. They're putting up directional signs out there and sending out direct mailers. The problem is not only that homebuyers forget about the postcard or directional sign 3 houses down. They are looking for more resources and content to assist their buying process and it's your job to plug them in.

We have different moments of truths when marketing to homeowners and homebuyers. The first moment of truth typically happens when they go to your website and they directly fill out a form to contact you for a design consultation. The second moment of truth happens when they experience your process, your timeline, and your costs. By the time you've built that home for them or remodeled their kitchen, the third moment of truth happens when they share their experiences with other people and their friends and families refer you to their networks. What is missing for a lot of builders is inserting themselves at the zero moment of truth, the pre-shopping experience, and this has recently become a phenomenon in new modern buyer behavior.

So the question is, are you tackling the zero moment of truth for your buyers? You need to be an authority in your industry by providing content for your buyers so that they can have a pre-shopping experience. This content should be on your own properties like your website, blog, and social media platforms. These platforms need to be interconnected in such a way that no matter where a buyer lands, they'll ultimately be led back to your hub, or website. If you can provide content on these properties, then you can really fulfill that pre-shopping experience.

The ultimate scenario is that by the time buyers are ready for the purchase at the first moment of truth, they're well and ready to engage with your team, with the added bonus they they have already built enough trust in you.

Google recently conducted research with Shopper's Science, where consumers were surveyed regarding how much content they consumed before making purchases in various industries and categories. The results of the survey showed that generally, the more expensive your service, the more content that is needed for them to consume before doing business with you.

Are you winning trust at the zero moment of truth? That is the question. This is the void that exceptional digital marketing should fill. Smart buyers no longer read the yellow pages to find a contractor because everything is now researched online.

The key to the buyer's heart is your ability to empower that buyer to make a better, informed decision. When you have this concept down, then you can follow a series of steps to attract strangers to your website, convert those website visitors into leads, close those leads into clients using automated technologies, and delight those clients to the point where they can't wait to refer you to others in their network.

Would you like to access our fast-start marketing bundle for builders and remodelers?

You'll get instant access to cheat sheets and guides that will fast-track you towards running your own marketing engine. Plus receive updates on my best marketing advice and a complimentary consultation offer where we'll map out the exact strategy to help you reach your goals.

Visit www.inboundmill.com/book-bundle

or text your first name and email address to (424) 652-6242

CHAPTER 4
Pay Per Click Vs. Getting Free Clicks

You have to understand not just what your customers need, but how and where they prefer to access information.

-Jay Baer

Traditional homebuilders spend money on marketing.

Smart builders invest money in marketing.

Traditional homebuilder online marketing relies on marketing spends, meaning there are no long term benefits to marketing dollars. If a builder wants more sales he must typically spend more time, more money or both, generating activity at the top of the sales funnel.

Smart builders view marketing budgets differently and invest in a marketing program that generates dividends over time in the form of new leads, appointments, and sales. Instead of spending money on temporary marketing methods to drive the next sale, smart builders create leverage against large builders by creating long term marketing assets that build relationships over time.

Before you ask yourself whether or not you should invest in paid advertising or any other form of marketing like SEO or direct mail, you should understand the 4 types of media. There are 4 types of digital media; Rented, paid, owned and earned. All four are important to your marketing plan, but the thing is, that traditional builder marketing focuses on rented and paid media. And a smart builder knows to primarily focus only on owned and earned media.

So here's how we break down the different forms of media and how they work within your online marketing strategy.

Rented Media

The first type of media which is rented media, refers to websites that are owned and controlled by someone else, but that you populate with your own content. Rented media websites include Facebook, Google Plus, Pinterest, Houzz, Twitter, Slideshare, Flicker and Tumblr among others. To understand rented media, consider renting versus owning real estate. For example, when you rent an apartment, someone else makes the rules. When you own, you make the rules. When you rent an apartment, you're making someone else rich and when you own real estate you're building your own asset.

Rented media works similarly. When the foundation of your online marketing is based on social networking sites such as Houzz, Facebook and Twitter, you're populating someone else's site. You don't own your own content and you're limited by someone else's rules about how you communicate with your audience, such as the way you must communicate within the confines of a user's profile on Houzz or Facebook.

Rented media is also very temporary.

In addition to the limited time and reach of each post you make on Facebook, rented media is also filled with distractions, updates from friends and families, ads, game requests, photos and videos. When you're on Pinterest you may be able to showcase your remodeling work but it's very easy for someone to get distracted and click on a picture of a cooking recipe. So the biggest risk by far in building a digital strategy is lead ownership. When someone follows your page on a rented media website, you don't own that lead and you don't control the frequency, the format, or the length of how you can follow up with that lead.

An email list of engaged leads and prospects is your most important online marketing assessment. Builders that build an audience on social media at the expense of building an email list are not building an asset; they are simply renting. Therefore, rented media must play only a supporting role in your online marketing strategy.

Paid Media

Paid media consists of paid advertising on Google, often referred to as Google Adwords. There are also other platforms that have acquired huge audiences which allow you to advertise to segments that you define. Facebook and Houzz are also really popular ways to reach an audience. Paid media is great. It's fast, immediate, and has its advantages:

- Often easy to setup

- Creates an immediate influx of website traffic

Let's define the risks associated with paid media:

- Since it has an auction-style format, you are also bidding against other builders and remodelers for the same audience

- The type of buyer clicking on your listing is often lower in quality than in organic searches

- Once you stop paying for ads, there's no ongoing benefit

Since this strategy doesn't build you an asset, it's not a long term solution. It does, however, serve as a great supplement to your online strategy.

Owned Media

This is the type of media that pays dividends in the form of long term leads and sales. You own it with 100% control and you set the rules for format as well as the type of content and visuals you want to show. Moreover, you are not competing with other ads or builders selling to the same audience.

Some examples of owned media are:

- Website

- Blog

- Landing Pages

- Ebooks

- Photos

The major benefit with owned media is that when you acquire a lead through your website or blog, you have 100% control of that lead and you are free to control the type of messaging that goes out to this lead. Another benefit is that owned media continually drives traffic back to itself.

If you've ever read a how-to-article online, you most likely have come across a company's blog. Each of those articles represents an individual asset that shows up in the search engines when someone types a keyword into Google. As you can imagine, the more topics a company writes about, the more real estate that company owns on the web that drives traffic back to their website.

Earned Media

Earned media is about earning the media's attention. This typically happens when you gain enough traction with your owned media that you're a force to be reckoned with. This includes articles that rank high in the search engines and positive feedback shared about you on websites like Yelp. It also includes other articles mentioning your company that get shared across the internet, which bring you more website traffic independent of you.

Some examples include:

- Reviews on Houzz

- Remarkable blog posts that rank high in the search engines

- Videos that get shared on Youtube

- Press releases that generate buzz about your company

How do you earn this media? By being client-centric with the content you produce and leveraging your high customer satisfaction rating on all of the different web properties online.

In short, if you have a big budget, paid media can take you very far. Depending on where you are with your active lead list, you may want to weigh the different types of media that make sense for your current situation.

Large lead list? Start budgeting for owned and earned media.

Small lead list? Start budgeting for paid media and work your way up to owned and earned media.

Would you like to access our fast-start marketing bundle for builders and remodelers?

You'll get instant access to cheat sheets and guides that will fast-track you towards running your own marketing engine. Plus receive updates on my best marketing advice and a complimentary consultation offer where we'll map out the exact strategy to help you reach your goals.

Visit www.inboundmill.com/book-bundle

or text your first name and email address to (424) 652-6242

CHAPTER 5
The Napkin $5,000 Quarterly Marketing Plan

The only thing worse than being blind is having sight but no vision.

-Helen Keller

Just as your financial portfolio should be reviewed and reallocated every 90 days, your online assets should be rebalanced as well. You should review shifts in your sales funnel to reveal which areas need specific focus as well as which marketing activities has and has not been working.

Think of your annual sales goals as your general destination and your quarterly digital marketing plan as your street by street GPS.

Your destination always stays the same but if you're blown off course, your quarterly plan can redirect you back on track. It's a live document that should always be updated, tweaked, measured and stay progressive. There's no single right way to do online marketing in the housing industry.

Every builder and remodeler has different strengths and weaknesses: you may have a small e-mail list, you may have no social media following, or you may have zero online reviews on Google Plus, but ten reviews on Houzz. You also may have an extensive video library but no professional photography shot with your last ten homes. These data points should all be documented with a SWOT analysis.

Seek to identify the strengths, weaknesses, threats and opportunities that you have before you and remember that a SWOT analysis can and does change constantly and should be reviewed every 90 days.

An inbound marketing agency typically charges around $5,000 to create a 90 day marketing strategy for you. If you have the time and talent in house to create this type of document, these are the basics of what you'll want to include:

What Are Your 90 Day Goals?

Indicate your specific business goals for the next 90 days. Do you want to sell 12 homes within that time frame?

How Will You Reach Those Goals?

Once you have your high level goals, break those goals down into specific, actionable objectives for each stage of the sales funnel.

Let's take a look at a very basic funnel:

Do you plan to increase your website visitors to leads with a conversion rate of 2% in the next 90 days? Do you also want to increase your lead to close rate in the next 90 days?

Who Are You Targeting In The Next 90 Days?

Who in the next 90 days are you specifically going to focus on in terms of buyer personas, or buyer profiles that are most likely to buy based on your 90 day inventory? You may have several homes that need to be closed within the next 90 days, so focusing on a specific buyer profile in order to close those homes just in time for Fall may be in your best interest.

Here is an example of a sample builder with a set of strengths, weaknesses, opportunities and threats.

John requires a certain tool set and set of tactics to attract and engage potential clients. He is a small volume custom builder that currently builds five homes per year and wants to increase that to twenty homes within a year. His business has been based on referrals for many years and now he needs to reach a new market to achieve his goal.

With his referral based business, John has not invested any time in online marketing. He has a static website, a Facebook page with only two page likes, a Twitter profile with less than 50 followers, and no blog. He has not invested in any professional photography for any of his projects, so his available resources to showcase his work are limited. However, he does have more than 20 testimonials in letter form. He also has a small email list of about 100 leads. He sends an email to this list once per quarter.

Now let's take a look at his strengths, weaknesses, opportunities and threats.

The strengths that he does have are that he has positive reviews and a positive product. His weaknesses are that he has a small existing audience, a static website that doesn't convert visitors into leads, very limited photography and a limited budget. What are his opportunities? He can leverage testimonials embedded in photography to show how he creates a dream home for families they all love and his threats are that he has limited brand recognition in the market, which could lead to longer sales cycles as buyers take longer to establish trust.

In order to create a 90 day objective for John, we need to consider what he wants to accomplish in the next 90 days. So let's say he needs 5 in-person appointments in the next 90 days. What he needs to do in terms of an action plan to meet his sales goals is to make and build interest quickly with potential clients online. Since he doesn't have an existing base of leads, he'll need to attract new leads into the top of the sales funnel, convert visitors to leads, establish a lead nurturing email campaign that nurtures leads quickly to in-person consultations.

Here's a napkin overview of what his marketing plan could look like:

In order to attract website visitors, he needs to set up a blog and commit to a schedule of 8 posts per month that will be promoted on social media channels and show up in local search results. He needs to write for his buyer persona that he's targeting in the next 90 days. What kinds of questions do these prospective clients immediately have that he can answer in 500 word posts? John can also leverage his photo website embed feature which he has available from his Houzz account to demonstrate custom home possibilities.

To engage with these potential prospects, he needs to increase his website to lead conversion by creating a free ebook download about the process of building a custom home. Adding a call to action to the side of the website and the bottom of every blog post will allow him to capture these leads, inviting these visitors to subscribe to the blog.

He can also add a blog subscriber opt-in form to the most popular website pages including his Floor Plans page, Photo Galleries page, or Virtual Tours page. He can also ask his existing clients if they would be willing to do a video testimonial, so that he could post these testimonials on his website.

Trust is a powerful factor in helping him convert his website visitors into leads. Finally, in order to lock in the influence, he should establish an email schedule every week to reach out to his existing lead list and identify active leads. He'll send out emails as he publishes new blog posts, igniting positive interest and conversation around his goodwill.

Would you like to access our fast-start marketing bundle for builders and remodelers?

You'll get instant access to cheat sheets and guides that will fast-track you towards running your own marketing engine. Plus receive updates on my best marketing advice and a complimentary consultation offer where we'll map out the exact strategy to help you reach your goals.

Visit www.inboundmill.com/book-bundle

or text your first name and email address to (424) 652-6242

CHAPTER 6
The Most Important Web Tools You'll Need

Take up one idea. Make that one idea your life- think of it, dream of it, live on that idea. Let the brain, muscles, nerves, every part of your body, be full of that idea, and just leave every other idea alone. This is the way to success.

-Swami Vivekananda

Creating success online is not about utilizing the latest technology, having the most expensive systems, or having the best vocabulary of acronyms to know what you're talking about. Like everything in life, the simplest of systems work best. The last thing you want to be doing is getting frustrated with technology. At the end of the day, there are countless numbers of tools that help facilitate your digital marketing activities.

We must remember that technology doesn't drive revenue; good business does, or at least good business assets. That said, here are some essential tools that every builder and remodeler should have. You can have additional tools based on your product, your audience and goals. But these tools will provide you the framework for success online.

Website and CMS

The first thing you need is a responsive website with CMS.

CMS stands for Content Management System.

Wordpress is one of the most popular CMS platforms out there. Investing in a website doesn't mean you have to spend tens of thousands of dollars. I've seen forty-thousand dollar websites from high-end agencies that converted less than 1% of website traffic to leads, and I've also seen three hundred dollar websites convert as high as 8%.

Here is what you must have for your website. It must be mobile-responsive. With an estimated 90% of shoppers starting their search online today, your website is essentially your online sales office. Just as you wouldn't equip your sales office with transistor radios and rotary phones, it's important not to rely on outdated technology. Responsive websites make it easy for potential home shoppers to get the information that they need whether they are browsing your website on an iPhone, laptop, or a tablet.

Your website also needs to have a CMS. Think of your website as a living, breathing thing that evolves and continues to grow. What a content management system will allow you to do is to give you the tools necessary to keep it living, breathing and evolving. You need to have fresh content, fresh photos, fresh videos, new landing pages and all these things can be easily added if you have a content management system.

For small owners, hiring an expensive in-house IT team or outsourcing every single website update is cost prohibitive. If you want to maintain your agility required to gain leverage on these big markets, you need to get hands on with your website. A CMS will afford you to do so. It will enable you and your team who may or may not necessarily be tech savvy, to change the copy, the photos, the videos, the blog posts and any other aspect of your website without any headaches.

I would recommend the Wordpress platform for websites, but there are also many choices available such as HubSpot.

HubSpot gives you more additional bells and whistles and it truly is an efficient, all-in-one-solution for your digital marketing needs.

Blog

The next tool that you need is a blog. A self-updated blog updated at least 8 times a month with content that's optimized for the search engines will create an automated prospecting tool to attract new leads to your website, 24 hours a day, 7 days a week. Your blog is your second biggest marketing asset after your email list. Every post that you publish using SEO-friendly content will pay dividends in the form of new leads for weeks, months or even years after each post is published.

Your blog is owned content. Remember that. This means that every visitor who opts in as a blog subscriber is an owned lead. A blog subscriber is also a high quality lead because they are agreeing to receiving emails every time you publish your new blog post.

Email Service Provider

The third thing you need is an email service provider. If you know that your email list is your number one, biggest asset you know that you need to start sending emails. People who have already signed up to receive emails are more likely to buy than somebody who follows you on social media or someone visiting your website for the first time.

Email marketing leverages all components of your marketing advantage. Email gives you immediate feedback about which prospects are actually engaging with the topics that they are interested in, which ebook offers are the most effective, and much, much more. Plus, it's never been easier, faster or more affordable to create more professional looking email campaigns. And with email, you can immediately respond to changes in the market, local or national news , and other factors that influence a potential homebuyer's decision.

Remember that email is your own media and you can distribute remarkable and authoritative content to help them make better decisions in doing business with you. If you're on a limited budget, look for the email service provider with easy to use design tools that don't require any specialized technical skill.

There are a lot of email service providers that offer drag and drop design tools, which allow you to design and send an email quickly, so that shouldn't be problem.

The next thing you need is CRM integration because your email service provider should offer easy integration with your CRM. Basically, when someone registers on your website or blog, the information automatically uploads to your CRM tool. This saves countless hours of data entry and reduces the risk of new leads falling between the cracks.

Having a CRM simply allows you to manage your contacts and visualize where your leads are at every stage of the sales funnel.

Autoresponders

You also need autoresponders because you may not have a team of online sales counselors who can respond to your new online lead within minutes.

What an autoresponder does is help you deliver those emails automatically when a website visitor registers.

When a sales team member cannot respond immediately to a prospective buyer, a well-written autoresponder can communicate a personalized welcome message. Autoresponders give you the confidence that you need in knowing that each new lead is getting touched even when teams are swamped.

CRM

A fifth tool that you should have is a CRM.

It's a key component of your raw strategy because a CRM can serve as a compass for your 90-day annual sales goals by providing information about your prospect quality, especially where your prospects are in the sales funnel. And it also helps you identify the lifetime value of your customers so you'll be better able to know important things such as how long it took for that website visitor to close to contract. You want to be able to close the loop on your marketing and a CRM will allow you to do that.

There are several home builder-specific CRM tools like Lasso Data Systems, but if your budget is tight, there are numerous low-cost and no-cost solutions available. Whether you decide to invest in an industry-specific solution or try a low-cost version, the most important thing is to set up a CRM of some kind to gain a better understanding of your buyers even if it means using Excel.

Google Analytics

You need to capture your data to glean insights from it. Enter Google Analytics. This is a very essential tool. It is basically a free tracking system that Google provides you. It's easy to install on your website and blog. Google Analytics is a very robust program that offers a lot of data, but keep in mind that Google Analytics can also give you more data than you need. It takes a pair of trained eyes to be able to gather insight from the right data.

In terms of getting the right data, we're talking about total number of visitors to your website, which ones were actually unique visitors, the average time they spent on your website, and the average number of pages they viewed when they visited your website, just to name a few important metrics.

This is all data that you can look at today inside of your Google Analytics platform.

As an advanced tip that actually should be mandatory to implement, you should learn how to set up goal tracking for your website. If you have a contact form on your Contact Us page, then you can track how many times a person has filled out that form month over month. I've seen too many profiles inside Google Analytics that don't have goal tracking implemented. Goal Tracking is necessary because it tells you how well you're converting your website visitors to leads. If you have Google Analytics right now, make it a point to set up goal tracking.

Would you like to access our fast-start marketing bundle for builders and remodelers?

You'll get instant access to cheat sheets and guides that will fast-track you towards running your own marketing engine. Plus receive updates on my best marketing advice and a complimentary consultation offer where we'll map out the exact strategy to help you reach your goals.

Visit www.inboundmill.com/book-bundle

or text your first name and email address to (424) 652-6242

CHAPTER 7
2 Questions: How Long and How Much?

If you genuinely want something, don't wait for it. Teach yourself to be impatient.

-Gurbaksh Chahal

Inbound marketing is a term and methodology used to describe a holistic digital marketing strategy to get customers online.

It involves a series of steps that a company must take in order to attract strangers as website visitors, convert those website visitors into leads, nurture those leads into clients using automated technology, and delight those clients into promoters of your brand.

At the end of the day, inbound marketing is a buzzword. However, it's a buzzword that will inevitably become the defacto standard for doing business online in the future.

Inbound marketing as a core part of your overall marketing strategy requires some degree of investment if you want to grow your company to its fullest extent on the web. If you want to generate leads and sales online, you've got to be ready to commit a sizeable portion of your marketing budget solely to inbound marketing. So, what does a full inbound plan cost and how does spending less or more affect the results that a company can see?

When it comes to setting aside a financial budget for inbound you truly do get what you pay for. The more you financially commit, the more tools, features and content you can have access to, in order to effectively convert your audience. So, we're going to take a look at several elements of an inbound plan that contribute to that cost for a total annual budget as well as how the relative size of your business can contribute as well.

Building an active social media presence on social media platforms such as Facebook, Linkedin, Twitter and Houzz can be the most useful tools for your business's inbound arsenal. For the best results you're going have to commit time and effort into maintaining a consistent active social media presence.

There's also visual content.

Content goes well beyond simple blogging. Custom infographics, design elements and action-oriented calls to action on your website can all be used to convey information and engage your audience.

There's also platform integration.

Full content integration with marketing platforms such as Hubspot is very standard practice for companies looking to expand on the web using analytics tools, lead management capabilities, and integration with other services such as your CRM.

These platforms are all invaluable to your inbound strategy. That said, these services all contribute an additional $200 to $2400 to your monthly inbound cost. Also keep in mind that blogging and lead management alone make up anywhere from $20-$30,000 of annual inbound marketing costs.

For the best online performance results, you should definitely commit a sizeable portion of your total marketing budget to inbound, through setting aside 8-10% of your total yearly revenue for marketing.

For instance, you should definitely consider setting aside about 25%-40% of that budget solely for inbound marketing strategies. The quality of leads you can generate with inbound marketing is going to be much, much higher than those hooked in with outbound techniques.

The total cost of inbound marketing for your company is also determined by how much more business you want to attract via inbound, how much you plan to grow, how much funding you're able to reasonably commit to inbound based on the percentage of your annual revenue. So the type of average budgets a company should set aside for inbound marketing should be categorized by the business size and determined by yearly revenues.

For more aggressive high return campaigns, companies should expect to spend an additional 30-50% of these amounts. If you're a local builder or a remodeler, consider spending about $40,000-$75,000 towards inbound marketing. If you're a larger builder or remodeler, then consider spending about $75,000-$200,000 towards inbound marketing.

For the best use of your marketing dollars, many companies partner up with professional inbound marketing agencies where they offer all-inclusive package deals that include all the various elements of inbound that I just mentioned. This is because in-house and freelance work really compiles quickly and can wind up costing far more than the figures you expect.

So, how long does it take to see results from inbound marketing?

Now, unless you spend a lot on ad buys or get featured on Extreme Home Makeover there are very few quick fixes or overnight success tactics in marketing. To really succeed it takes time, effort, funding and consistency. Inbound marketing is really no exception. To really see the long term benefits from inbound marketing it takes time.

How much time? Well, just like many things, the short answer is, it depends. Inbound marketing is a marathon, not a sprint. It takes months of foundational work and strategy to plant the right seeds and get the proper return on investment.

Let's take a look at some examples:

Here's an example of website traffic analytics for a remodeling company doing inbound marketing.

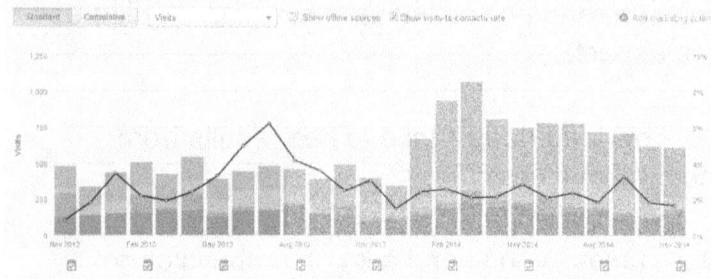

Now, as you can see the increase has been slow and steady overtime, but has resulted in a 2x increase in website traffic over 24 months.

In this particular case, the company was blogging about 4 times a month and generating content at a very slow pace. They saw strong lead conversions on their website at a healthy 2% visit to lead conversion rate.

By increasing the pace of content generation, they would begin to see even faster results and that's exactly what they did in 2014; with a push on content optimization they drove up traffic while maintaining strong conversions.

Let's take a look at a solid surface countertop company.

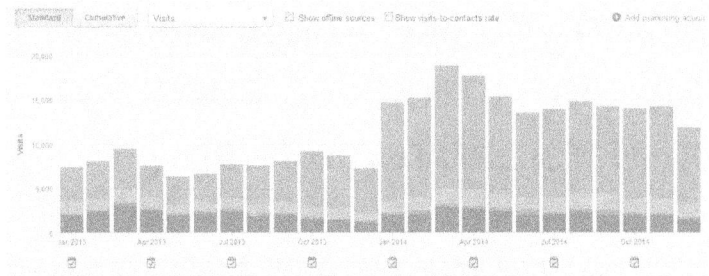

Now what did they do differently? Well, this company invested in an inbound marketing program that included weekly blogging, and a more aggressive content generation schedule. They have ebook offers being produced every other month at a minimum and as a result, they're seeing faster results that are much, much more dramatic.

So, what does this mean for your organization? The bottom line is, the more you invest, the faster you go. You shouldn't expect consistent results for at least 6 months. Of course, measurable results will be seen month over month and you'll be able to predict your future quarters based on data. Work with your agency to get content improved and published quickly, or your results can be stifled. Also keep in mind that that there are always exceptions, and you might be that case.

Would you like to access our fast-start marketing bundle for builders and remodelers?

You'll get instant access to cheat sheets and guides that will fast-track you towards running your own marketing engine. Plus receive updates on my best marketing advice and a complimentary consultation offer where we'll map out the exact strategy to help you reach your goals.

Visit www.inboundmill.com/book-bundle

or text your first name and email address to (424) 652-6242

CHAPTER 8
Differentiation Produces Quality Clients

Progress is measured by the degree of differentiation within a society.

-Herbert Read

There's two significant components to differentiating your brand. The first part is to focus on an ideal client and that requires developing a buyer persona for this type of person. The second part is to find some way to clearly differentiate your business with your unique value proposition.

Buyer Persona Development

When you lack a niche focus for the type of clients you want to attract, you end up being all things to all people. Do some research on who your best clients are and seek to understand them. Developing a buyer persona should serve as the first step towards building your marketing strategy.

Basically, a buyer persona is a fictional representation of your ideal client.

- Ask yourself these questions:

- How do they evaluate other companies like yours?

- What does your persona value most?

- What are their pain points?

- What are their common objections?

- What does the typical day look like for your ideal client?

It also helps that you interview your current clients or better yet, your prospective clients that you lost in the past. It's a good idea to ask them these same questions. Find the commonalities among your client base by conducting interviews with them. Focus on their decision criteria and how they began their research prior to finding your directional sign or talking to their friend who referred you.

The more accurate your developed buyer persona is, the more successful any of your online marketing will be thereafter. When you identify the right buyer personas, you can give them names like "Green Conscious Larry" or "Family Man Barry". Anything you do online and the content you put out will be targeted and written for these personas.

Unique Value Proposition

Once upon a time, an architect was asked what he did for a living. "I'm an architect. I design buildings," he replied. When pressed further, he bragged, "No one else knows how to design a building like I do."

Yet, when the architect's customers were asked what he did, they said, "We expected good design. But let me tell you what he really does. He helps us cut through all the City Hall red tape and that gets us paid faster."

His three customers all said essentially the same thing. Now when asked what he does for a living, the architect replies, "I help you get paid faster. Sure, I'm an architect, but I also help you cut through City Hall red tape. I'm the contractor's architect."

By embracing his new message, the architect's business went from a second or third tier player to the #1 commercial architect in his market.

That's the power of differentiation.

So the other part of differentiating your brand is through your unique value proposition. What is different about you from your client's point of view? Can I pull up four different builder websites, blur out the branding and photography, and identify your company from the text alone? A lot of builders can talk about their custom home process and sound very similar to each other. Your process may not be what really sets you apart from your competition.

The good news is that your clients know exactly why you are different. When you have answers to questions like, "What made you desire to hire us? What's the one thing than we can do better than others like us? And would you refer us or do you refer us?", you'll be ahead of your competition in spades. Also, don't assume you know what this differentiation is until you hear it from the mouths of your clients.

Identify your unique value proposition. Without this differentiation, your content will flounder and take you twice as long to gain traction with your online audience.

Would you like to access our fast-start marketing bundle for builders and remodelers?

You'll get instant access to cheat sheets and guides that will fast-track you towards running your own marketing engine. Plus receive updates on my best marketing advice and a complimentary consultation offer where we'll map out the exact strategy to help you reach your goals.

Visit www.inboundmill.com/book-bundle

or text your first name and email address to (424) 652-6242

CHAPTER 9
How Many Consultations Does It Take?

Storms make trees take deeper roots.

-Dolly Parton

Times have changed in the last 5 years where buyer behavior has changed dramatically. People no longer flip through the yellow pages to find a contractor who they can know, like and trust.

Today, buyers search for information online in order to empower themselves to make a better decision. But how many of them are there?

More importantly, what is the minimum amount of qualified traffic you need to get in front of to get the amount of consultations you need to reach your goals?

If you want to know how many buyers in your geographic area are actually online searching for services in your industry, a very good way to do that is to look into Google's search data. Google shows you the number of times per month your clients are actually searching for residential contractors in your area. You just have to know what those keywords are.

For instance, if you're a custom home builder a very common keyword that has a lot of buyer intent behind it is something like "custom home builders tampa fl". Or another variation of the same keyword, but with a separate volume of searches like "tampa custom home builders".

Let's get an idea of what kind of numbers we're looking at here:

In Nashville, the keyword "custom home builders" has about 110 average searches per month. There are 280 searches in Tampa, FL, 480 searches in Austin, TX, 210 searches in Denver, CO, and 720 searches in Houston, TX.

What you should also realize is that there's buyer intent behind many more keywords if you're a custom home builder. There are keywords such as "new home builders", "new home construction", or "custom home process" that when combined could help you optimize your marketing efforts for a larger market share. The search volume for all of these keywords put together can potentially add up to a lot of people searching for your services. Again, it's all about starting with keyword research and if you were to show up on the first page of Google for any or all these keywords, you have the potential to really get a good grasp on your local or regional markets.

Remember, people are actually going onto Google. com and searching for these services due to having a need for them at that particular time. So, the probability of you turning them into a lead is very high. But Google search volume isn't the only place where there are interested buyers.

There are also websites that have accumulated large audiences in your industry, which is exactly why these companies have such high valuations. Let's take Twitter for example. Twitter is a fascinating social media platform. If you were to advertise on Twitter, they'd give you the data, broken down by demographics and user behavior, so that you can hone in on your exact audience that you want to target in your geographic area.

Now, Twitter is ubiquitous, like Tom Brady, Carrie Underwood, and Coke Zero. Twitter is almost universally on the radar of Americans. 87% of respondents have heard of Twitter compared to 88% who have heard of Facebook. While only 7% of Americans are using, the Twitter population is still 17 million people which is roughly equivalent to the combined population of Connecticut, Oregon, Kentucky, Kansas, and Oklahoma.

And while substantially smaller than the Facebook brigade, the Twitter crew is tuned into brands like nowhere else on the social web.

The way I see Twitter is like this: Twitter is a great place for people to connect quickly and have a chat with each other. For business purposes, this is also where influencers are having conversations about the topics at large. If you were to target influencers on Twitter, it would be very easy to do so because all tweets are made publicly available and you could enter keywords to find the conversation you want to be a part of. Twitter segues nicely into a deeper connection and conversation on Facebook.

Now, you would be wasting your time on Twitter if you were not actively engaging and interacting in real-time. According to survey results, 53% of Twitter users never post any updates. To me, this re-emphasizes the needs to be keyword smart in your tweets and not to dip into the pool of banality. Even though half of your clients may not be tweeting or retweeting, they are watching, reading, and retweeting, so take the opportunity to post valuable content that lead back to your website.

Pinterest is a great platform for builders, remodeling firms and everyone else in the built environment. If you have great photography to showcase, Pinterest is the next best platform to display it next to Houzz. Unlike Houzz, however, Pinterest can distract users from paying attention to your great work because there are also cooking recipes competing for real estate.

1/3 of all Pinterest signups come from men. Pinterest is notoriously known for attracting the female dominated user base. 71% of Pinterest users are women, but usage demographics are slowly changing. In 2014 the number of men using Pinterest doubled. This creates an opportunity for brands looking to reach male and female consumers.

For builders and remodelers, Pinterest provides an opportunity to insert yourself in the decision making process in the household due to the fact that wives on Pinterest are typically swaying the decisions.

Do people on Pinterest actually turn into buyers? The answer is a resounding yes. 93% of Pinterest users shopped online in the past 6 months. An older study found women tend to use Pinterest as a wish list, while men use the platform as a shopping cart.

Still though, this is a great opportunity to convert website visitors into blog subscribers coming from Pinterest.

Blog subscribers can be nurtured into a point of sales engagement. I would recommend that you set the geographic location for every pin you place on Pinterest. There's nothing worse than a Pinterest user who wants to contact the company immediately only to click on a broken link or be taken to an unrelated page, or even a page for a contractor who lives a hundred-miles away from them. Make sure that your pins lead to pages where buyers can get more information and take action.

There are countless niche social networks out there these days where some are finding more success than others. But there is not a better focused directory and social media platform for attracting homeowners and homebuyers than Houzz.

Houzz is an online community, directory, and marketplace for all things home designs, whether you're building, remodeling, redecorating or just dreaming. Houzz offers a great deal of assistance and inspiration.

The number of local professionals on Houzz adds up to around 500,000 professionals. The number of Houzz users adds up to around 25 million users. The percentage of Houzz that are between the ages of 25 to 54 is 72%. Make sure that you have the right focus on what you offer when you choose a category on Houzz. If you mostly do kitchen remodels, your best bet is to be in the kitchen remodeling category rather than the design build category.

As you can see, when you combine your marketing efforts on social media and Google search, you should have absolutely no problem with having a large audience to constantly nurture. As long as you can reach a minimum amount of traffic needed to produce the amount of appointments needed to reach your goals, you're all set.

Would you like to access our fast-start marketing bundle for builders and remodelers?

You'll get instant access to cheat sheets and guides that will fast-track you towards running your own marketing engine. Plus receive updates on my best marketing advice and a complimentary consultation offer where we'll map out the exact strategy to help you reach your goals.

Visit www.inboundmill.com/book-bundle

or text your first name and email address to (424) 652-6242

CHAPTER 10
Cracking The First Page of Google

The question isn't who is going to let me; it's who is going to stop me.

-Ayn Rand

To succeed with search engine optimization and rank for keywords you care about, it's necessary to understand how Google works. Google does two basic things.

First, it crawls the internet looking for web pages, storing these web pages in its index. Think of the Google index as a massive catalog much like a library would have a catalog of every book.

Second, it has software that processes user searches and finds the best matching webpages in its index.

Google needs to crawl and index a web page. If your web page isn't even crawled, you're not even in the race. Then, of all the possible web pages that Google thinks is a match for the word being researched or being searched, your page or pages have to be considered better than the other possible candidates.

Getting Google to index a web page is not as hard to do as it once was. You see, in the early days of SEO, it was often necessary to manually submit new web pages to Google and the other search engines so they would know these pages existed. Many SEO consultants and software tools offer this as a service called search engine submission.

Today, a manual web page submission is rarely necessary. Instead, simply getting a link to a new webpage from a page that's already been crawled by Google is sufficient to get the new page crawled as well. That's how most of the Google index gets into the pages on Google today.

If you do decide to manually submit your page to Google, it's free and easy and should not involve hiring a consultant. Just use the Google Add URL tool at google.com/adurl. Getting a web page indexed by Google is not the problem; getting a web page to rank well is the challenge. To understand how to rank well, it's important to understand the basics of how the Google algorithm works.

So let's dig in into how Google's software brain works. I promise I won't make it too technical and you'll know enough to impress your friends at the next cocktail party. When a user types a keyword in the Google search box, Google first looks into its billions of indexed pages and comes up with a list of results that are matches for the term. For example, if you type "inbound marketing" into the Google search box, there are currently about a million and sixty thousand pages that Google finds related to that term. Once Google has this list of pages, it sorts the list so the highest quality results are at the top of the list and the lowest quality results are at the bottom.

Ranking is based on a combination of two things: relevance and authority.

The relevance is how close to a match a given webpage is to the term being searched. This is based on factors such as the title tag, sometimes the page title, the page content, and the anchor text of links to the page.

The authority of a page is a measure of how important and how authoritative that given page is in the eyes of Google. The authority of a web page is at the heart of the Google algorithm. Google call this Authority Page Rank, named after Larry Page, one of the founders of Google.

The idea behind Page Rank is brilliantly simple based on work at Stanford University on how to measure the credibility and the importance of academic papers. The authority of a given academic paper can be determined by the number of other papers that cited and referenced it.

The more citations a given paper has, the better the paper. However, not all citations are created equal.

A citation from another paper that itself has a higher number of citations is considered to carry more weight. Higher authority papers are cited by higher authority papers. It is the same principle that drives Google's Page Rank, but instead of academic papers, it's about web pages and instead of citations, it's about links from other web pages. The authority of a web page is based on the number of links by other web pages and the authority of those pages.

Here is a simple example.

Let's say you've created a web page about the best restaurants in Boston. If your page is just sitting there and no one is linking to it, Google assigns a relatively low authority score to your page. This is not surprising as Google has no evidence that you know what you're talking about or your content is of high quality. Overtime, other bloggers find your web page and link to it from their pages. This causes your authority to increase. The more powerful the pages that link to you, the more your authority goes up. Now if someday a link for the Boston Globe links to your page, your authority goes up significantly. Why? Because Boston.com itself, is a high authority website.

So to get SEO authority, the name of the game is to get as many links as possible from as many authority sites as possible. How do you get links? By creating remarkable content. Search engine optimization, when done well, is not about tricking Google into ranking your web page. It's about creating content that users would want to find, and helping Google deliver great search results.

The best way to rank well in the Google search results is to create content that is rank worthy. By rank worthy, we mean content that is worthy of being ranked because it is what the user who is searching would consider to be of high quality and relevance.

Here are some SEO stats:

- 60% of all organic clicks go to the organic top 3 results (Business 2 Community)

- SEO leads have a 14.6% close rate while outbound leads such as direct mail and print advertising have a 1.7% close rate (Search Engine Journal).

So what entails SEO work? Well, SEO starts with picking the perfect keywords that drive website visitors to your website. The first step of SEO is deciding which keywords to optimize your site for.

Keywords are what users type into the search box for a search query. Everything else can be broken down into 2 disciplines. The first is called On Page SEO and this refers to optimizing the content on your web page. The second one is called Off Page SEO, which refers to all the work you perform "off" of your website on the web.

On Page SEO

Let's first discuss On Page SEO. Once you've picked your list of target keywords, you want to optimize the content on your website you're trying to rank for to be readable by the search engines as well as the readers. These are factors that you can control directly by modifying your web pages and as such, are the easiest factors to address to improve your SEO.

The page title tag is the one element on your page that influences Google the most. It is the most important piece of the puzzle when doing On Page SEO. The page title is what shows up when you hover over the tab on your browser window and is used for the link display in search results.

Given the importance of the page title tag for SEO, it's worth spending a fair amount of time crafting great titles for your most important pages. The homepage of your website is a great way to start since it will eventually gain the most page authority. However, don't just stop there. Look for deeper pages in your website that are important and optimize the titles for those pages, too. For most businesses, especially home builders and remodelers, the traffic potential of these pages when added up is very significant.

A typical page title for a home builder would probably be "Custom Home Builders In Atlanta". If you're a home remodeler, your page title would be "Home Remodeling Contractors | Los Angeles, California". When Google's search spiders are crawling your site, they'll be able to recognize exactly what your website is about. For users browsing the list of search results, they'll know exactly what they'll be reading about if they click on your listing.

Similar to the page title, the meta description tag also provides information about a web page. It's usually a brief summary on what a user can expect to see on the webpage. Also, like the page title, the meta description is included in special HTML code on the page and isn't visible on the page with the rest of the content.

From an SEO perspective, the meta description doesn't directly influence your search rankings in any of the major search engines. What it does is provide a user a detailed description of what your page is about. The clearer your description is, the more likely users will click on your listing. A high click-through rate can indirectly boost your rankings because Google will determine that your web page is valuable to readers. A quick tip for writing your page descriptions is to keep it short and no more than 160 characters because Google truncates long descriptions.

Another element of On Page SEO is optimizing your URL. Every public resource on the internet has a unique URL which is basically the internet address of the page. In case you were wondering, URL stands for Uniform Resource Locator.

Most modern content management systems will let you customize URLs for your webpages, so if you're using a CMS like Wordpress, you can take advantage of the content management system to optimize your URL from an SEO's perspective. When Google crawls a web page, it looks at the URL as one of the factors it considers to determine the relevance of a webpage for a given keyword. If someone on Google is looking for the term, "custom home builders los angeles" and your page URL has that keyword in it, your URL sends a subtle signal to Google that it's likely what the page is about.

When other websites link to your website, they often just copy and paste a URL to their web pages and don't go through the trouble of specifying the anchor text. In these cases, the URL becomes the anchor text. If you have the target keywords in the URL itself, you'll have a higher chance of getting anchor text with those keywords when people link to your page.

So far, we've talked about the page title, meta description and the importance of optimizing your URL for the keyword you want to rank for. Now let's discuss the page content itself, the body of the page.

There are several considerations here to keep in mind here from an SEO perspective. When creating a web page, you can put headings in the page content, much like the headings in a book or newspaper article.

A heading on a web page is used to organize information and to help the content be easier to read. Even though some words have a font size that are big enough to look like a heading to people doesn't mean they look that way to Google. You must tag words on your page so they look like headings to the search engines.

A very common tactic for doing this is to use a single H1 header on each page as well as multiple H2 and H3 headers. If your page title is about kitchen remodeling services then you would want to wrap that heading around an H1 tag.

Many builder sites are image heavy. Images are a great way to illustrate a point and make your content more attractive and appealing. This is particularly true for long pieces of content that contain a lot of text. From an SEO perspective, one important thing to understand is that Google can't really see images or any text that's in the image. Google will not interpret the text embedded on those images.

A quick tip for checking if your images are readable by Google is to try to highlight the text with your mouse, as if you were going to copy and paste it. If you can't highlight the text, chances are it's an image and Google can't see it. To help with this, all important images on your web page should include what is known as an Alt Attribute. This is a special code that allows you to describe an image with text in a way that Google can see it. Also, like the URL of your web pages, the URL of your important images should contain your keywords.

Off Page SEO

Now, let's talk about Off Page SEO. It's the part of SEO that really matters and really moves the needle in helping you rank your keywords. Although the on page factors of SEO are important and relatively easy to do, if you want to make any significant improvements in your ranking, you're going to need to address off page factors as well.

Off page factors are not on the pages you control, but on other web pages. The most important off page factor is inbound links. An inbound link is a link on another page that points to your page. As discussed earlier, Google places a great deal of emphasis on the authority of a web page in determining search rankings. Authority is calculated based on the inbound links to your web page and the authority of those pages linking to it. The most effective way to get inbound links is by creating remarkable content that is useful and interesting. Getting inbound links is the most effective way to get better rankings on Google.

One way to get links from other people is to contact them and request that they link to your site. Another way is to create some content that you think is valuable to that person's readership. So if they have a website about kitchen storage ideas and you create some content around kitchen storage ideas that their readers would find really valuable, they would love the prospect of featuring your piece of content. When they feature your piece of content in the form of a guest article on their website, you can insert a link in your author byline that goes back to your website from that article.

Having said that, if you've created some exceptionally remarkable content that you think would be beneficial to the readers of a particular site or blog, it's fine to reach out to them. When reaching out to bloggers or site owners, make sure the email is highly personalized and demonstrate that you read their site and understand their audience.

Send a link to the content that you think would be relevant for them. Usually this is not your homepage, but a deeper page like a blog article. And finally, don't explicitly ask for a link. You're basically sharing information that you think might be useful; if they like it and think it would be interesting to their audiences, they might link to it.

Would you like to access our fast-start marketing bundle for builders and remodelers?

You'll get instant access to cheat sheets and guides that will fast-track you towards running your own marketing engine. Plus receive updates on my best marketing advice and a complimentary consultation offer where we'll map out the exact strategy to help you reach your goals.

Visit www.inboundmill.com/book-bundle

or text your first name and email address to (424) 652-6242

CHAPTER 11
Social Media Sounds Like A Waste of Media

Distracted from distraction by distraction.

-T.S. Eliot

Houzz is an online community and professional directory that brings together homeowners, homebuyers and service professionals in the built environment.

A design build remodeling client of mine asked me to jump on a call with his account representative over at Houzz. The agenda was to go over his past year's performance on Houzz to see what worked, what didn't work and how we were going to improve upon the activities he was doing in order to see better results.

Basically, by the end of the call I felt that the account representative was a little misleading in the way he directed the conversation.

What I felt was important wasn't being addressed and what I felt needed to be addressed was de-emphasized. You see, Houzz gives you an analytics report about your performance. You can see how many people added your photos to ideabooks as well as how many impressions your particular photos received within a timeframe.

If your business is not already in the habit of strategizing with the aid of monitored KPIs, then Houzz and every other social media network will always have the upper hand in up-selling you services you aren't ready for. The dashboard metrics were glazed upon at best by the account representative, and the direction of the conversation was focused entirely on adding more paid modules like mobile advertising to his account.

When you are marketing on Houzz, you need to have the basics down first. Focus on optimizing your photos with more keywords. Commit time to engaging with users and discussions. Upload your new photos on a regular basis. If you don't have these basics down, make it a point to get this part down.

Whichever social platform that you are using whether it be Twitter, Facebook or Houzz, there are metrics for those platforms that tell you whether or not your actions are improving and if the needle is being moved for your business.

92% of marketers agreed that social media is important for their business, up from 86% in 2013. Also, 80% of marketers indicated that their social media efforts increased traffic. The important thing to realize is that social media marketing alone will not drive up revenue for your business. It needs to be looked as an integrated part of your overall digital marketing strategy.

Social media should be viewed as an opportunity for you to socialize the content that you produce online. If you have a website, you have an opportunity to make that content on your website known to as many people as possible and social media affords you that opportunity.

When you can share your content to as many people as possible, you're able to get out the word that you do what you do. You see, luck has a lot to do with communicating what you do best, to as many people as possible. So when you're able to increase that surface area of your communication platform, the more luck you're going to have, the more leads you're going to have and the more qualified clients that you're going to have.

Social media is not a waste of time, but at the end of the day, it's just another platform for you to engage with people who want to listen and do business with you.

There's a right way and a wrong way to participate in social media.

The wrong way to participate is to directly sell your services. That sounds like this in a tweet, "Whoever needs kitchen remodeling services please contact 555-5555". The right way to do it is to educate your user base with remarkable content that empowers them to make a better decision to buy from you. When you are unbiased in the way you provide content through these social media platforms, people will get to know, like and trust you enough to eventually do business with you.

When you think about the millions of users on social media, you might be thinking of all the different people who comprise the gamut of the demographics in existence. You might be thinking of all the people in certain subsets who could be your potential clients. That's great if you have an advertising budget and are looking to dip into paid media.

The right way to think about social media when you are building owned and earned media is to think about the influencers of social media. How can you leverage their audiences to promote your services? This is the best way to reach bigger audiences. When you can leverage an influencer's audience you can tap into a large network that you could not tap into if you were just speaking to a homeowner living out in Kentucky, who might happen to be in the market for a bathroom remodel.

When you leverage an influencer's network who is known for talking about bathroom storage ideas and they eventually share your content about bathroom remodeling, then you have this trickle effect of reaching hundreds of thousands of people over time that will eventually be your eyes and ears and voice.

There are thousands of bloggers and publishers online who have niche topic expertise and it's up to your team to figure out who they are. Build relationships with influencers and you earn the right to market your product to as many people as possible.

There's a concept called socializing your content, and this is where blogging meets social media.

You can't be successful on social media without a content engine and you can't cost effectively promote your content without the existence of various free social media channels to market in.

Whenever you create your next blog post be sure that you publish it and then promote it on social networks such as Facebook, Twitter and Houzz. You're promoting it to thousands of users who will then share that content with their thousands of users. Without this network effect at play, your blog posts will just sit there and look pretty. Set your content up to get viral, but when I say make your content viral, I don't mean that it needs to be the best content in the world or even the most interesting content in the world.

If you can make your content interesting enough to be commented on, then you are taking your first step to socializing your content. A small comment on your blog can turn into a share on Twitter, which can then turn into thousands of shares on facebook, further leading to visits to your website.

Adam owned a remodeling firm in Philadelphia, but lacked a strong social media following. He had no Facebook followers, no Twitter followers, wasn't on Pinterest, and he was barely engaging on Houzz. Needless to say, he had no social media following. We had a goal to build targeted followers in local markets by educating people with remarkable content. We wanted them to share and comment on the content because these were actions that gave us the green light to create more in order to attract more prospects, leads and clients in the long run.

You have to build targeted followers so that when you create content and share it, people will actually listen. The last thing you want is your content to fall on deaf ears.

Each social media channel has its associated challenges. Twitter can easily be used to create followers as long as you stay engaged. Facebook is trickier because if your content isn't receiving any comments or shares, its algorithm will be quick to only show your content to a small percentage of the total number of fans on your business page. Success on Houzz is very reliant on exceptional photos and lots of reviews, in other words, credibility.

Our team began creating content on Adam's blog by blogging 8 times per month, twice a week. This gave us the content that we needed to start having something valuable to say. In addition, we had e-book offers that we created around those blog post topics. We had premium content offers to give away which covered areas like optimum value design, questions that you need to ask a remodeling contractor, and kitchen storage ideas for your home. These were all premium content offers that were shared in conjunction with our blog posts.

Socializing your blog posts happens when you publish your blog post and distribute it to social media for other people to have a conversation around it. We made it a point to promote his blog posts just as much as spending the time to create it. When you socialize your blog post to the point that people start to talk about it via commenting and sharing, you'll eventually drive traffic to your website where you can capture your visitors and turn them into leads. This is exactly what Adam was able to do as we built those targeted followers and socialized his blog posts.

What's your endgame when you create your blog posts and distribute it via social media? What do you want people in social media to do when they click on that link which leads them to that blogpost?

If your endgame is to capture them as a lead then you need to have a call to action at the end of your blog post. Your call to action at the end of your blog post can be a premium content offer. What that premium content offer is basically saying is, "Look, you just read 500 words about this topic of aging in place...would you like a more in-depth look at this particular topic that will help you further understand what you need to know?."

When you have these calls to action placed on your blog posts, every single website visitor coming from social media will have an action to take by the time they finish reading your blogpost. The starting point is your Facebook post and the finish line is the call to action leading to a form.

Would you like to access our fast-start marketing bundle for builders and remodelers?

You'll get instant access to cheat sheets and guides that will fast-track you towards running your own marketing engine. Plus receive updates on my best marketing advice and a complimentary consultation offer where we'll map out the exact strategy to help you reach your goals.

Visit www.inboundmill.com/book-bundle

or text your first name and email address to (424) 652-6242

CHAPTER 12
The Power In Broadcasting Your Company's Diary

You are what you share.

-Charles W. Leadbeater

Someone once asked me what blogging is. This is my attempt at a baseline answer: A blog is basically a frequently updated personal diary on your website. There are bloggers who have blogs with personal updated diaries on their websites. There are also companies that have blogs which are basically the same thing, except these blogs facilitate the company's thought leadership. So, as a company, your blog needs to facilitate your thoughts about the topics that matter to your target audience, like lot buying and home design.

The best way to think about blogging is to think about what questions your prospects are asking. What questions are homeowners and homebuyers asking frequently that lead to your services? When I create content plans for my clients for their blog, I typically start asking them what the triggers are that cause them to look for a company like theirs. These triggers typically lead to goals that your target buyer wants to accomplish. An answer to a question that helps bring them closer to this goal builds trust.

In the housing industry, a person experiences triggers like:

- "Our family is expanding and our home is too small"

- "We just moved to a new area and existing pre-built options are limited in design"

- "Our home equity has increased"

If a home buyer experiences one of these triggers, they would set out to achieve a goal that relates to that trigger. In this case the goals would be:

- "I need a home with more space"

- "I want a better quality home and quality finishings."

- "I want a space that accommodates for my updated lifestyle."

Effective content marketing begins with an understanding of these triggers and the various questions someone will need to answer in order to accomplish their goals.

A really common exercise that I use with my clients in arriving at the questions that their prospects are asking is this:

Imagine that you're a thought leader walking down the street. Someone recognizes you and blurts out a question as they walk past you. You both have somewhere important to go, but you still want to help. What is the simplest answer that would help them achieve their goal? This answer must be short and to the point without being brand specific.

Here's an example:

Prospect: "What is the difference between an architect and a design builder?"

You: "An architect could design to your heart's content while a design builder really has an incentive to both design and hand you the keys to your new home."

Now take your answer and go down a rabbit hole. If you and your prospect were given a little more time, what would your prospect logically ask as a follow up question to that answer? You should be able to come up with at least 5-10 questions. What you'll end up with is a series of questions around the topic of design build. You can turn each of these questions into catchy blog post titles.

Now think about this: Wouldn't your prospect type these questions into Google? When your blog post headline turns up with a thoughtful answer to that question, you have a strong chance of converting them from a website visitor into a lead, as long you have a call to action for them at the end of the blog post.

Blogging is about meeting your prospect where they are; it's about being a part of the conversation and empowering them to make a better decision. When you are able to answer questions that your prospects are asking online, you're seen as a thought leader and as a company they can know and trust enough to do business with you.

Here are 6 things you should know about business blogging:

1. Blogging is not an option for your business. As you already know, keeping a blog on your company's home page filled with industry news, insights, and informative content is beneficial for your business for many reasons. If you have a blog then you will have 67% more leads than those who don't. One of the benefits of blogging is being able to attract high quality leads even when you're not working. The more leads in contact with you, the more likely you are to make a sale. If you're putting out content on a consistent basis, you'll be surprised how much your older leads will re-engage with you. Even your older blog posts can get you noticed if they are still relevant.

2. Marketers who have prioritized blogging are 13X more likely to enjoy positive ROI. If you consistently blog, you'll reap the benefits. Blogging helps you get found online, it should be a core part of your search engine optimization strategy. Your reach from this alone will bring you leads that continue to pay dividends in the form of appointments and closed contracts.

3. By 2020, customers will manage 85% their relationships without talking to a human.
   This means that your prospects are more likely to do their own research about your company before your first point of contact with them. One of the easiest ways for them to learn about your company is through your blog. You can easily influence the way your visitors buy with the help of your blog.

4. The only thing blogging costs you: your time.
   You have opportunity costs to weigh against. Hiring content writers to do this for you is more important than ever. Outsource these tasks to an agency who can consistently produce fresh content for you.

5. Companies who blog receive 55% more visitors to their website.
   You see, producing reliable and insightful, industry news to your visitors, pays off. Not only would it increase your reputability, but it will also bring you more inbound links.

6. Blogs have been rated as the 5th most trusted source for accurate online information. Blogs by nature have a personal touch to them. For this reason, blogs serve as a great opportunity to extend your brand and showcase your personality, as well as your specific product: your homes and remodeling work.

A business blog shouldn't be overlooked. Without a doubt, traction takes longer than paid advertising, but keep a consistent, quality blog and you'll see the ripple effects it will have in your client acquisition efforts.

Would you like to access our fast-start marketing bundle for builders and remodelers?

You'll get instant access to cheat sheets and guides that will fast-track you towards running your own marketing engine. Plus receive updates on my best marketing advice and a complimentary consultation offer where we'll map out the exact strategy to help you reach your goals.

Visit www.inboundmill.com/book-bundle

or text your first name and email address to (424) 652-6242

CHAPTER 13
Inbound Marketing Is The New Marketing

Focus on the core problem that your business solves and put out lots of content and enthusiasm, and ideas about how to solve that problem.

-Laura Fitton

I'd like to talk to you about buyer personas. Now, a lot of companies and marketers understand the value of knowing who their target audiences are: the cars they drive, where they live, how much money they make per year, and so on. Unfortunately, this doesn't give us the data to drive smarter marketing campaigns. It doesn't tell our salespeople when they can better engage with your buyers at the right time.

Buyer persona development starts with understanding buyer behavior, as well as their needs and challenges. And it doesn't really stop at understanding what those demographics are because those demographics can be found in any analyst report. So, buyer persona development starts with an interview with your past client that explores their entire buying journey from hearing about you all the way up to the point of closing a contract with you.

You are seeking to understand priority initiatives, what triggered them to look for a solution like yours, and what the success factors were when they imagined your solution. We want to understand those perceived barriers they have, those pushbacks they have when considering your service and also more importantly, what their decision criteria were that allowed them to make an empowered decision to do business with you.

Once you are able to tie together the touch points in a prospective client's buying journey, you will have a smarter marketing campaign that really plays dividends in the form of long term leads and clients. With your buyer persona identified, you can now move forward with a content strategy that incorporates a home buyer's interests and needs.

Content is the backbone of your digital marketing strategy. The frameworks that hold this content are your website, your blog, your videos, and your photos. Without a complete understanding of your buyer personas, you won't be able to create compelling content that moves a prospective client down the sales funnel.

The main business objective used to be about building a website. Now the objective is utility. In other words, we must use our websites to facilitate content that helps your potential clients.

Enter inbound marketing.

This is how you turn your website into a sales tool that generates a consistent stream of leads and clients for your business:

Generate Traffic To Your Website

Companies who blog get 70% more leads than those who don't. Now, how much should you be blogging? Well, more than you probably are right now. Make sure to follow these 5 blogging best practices:

Strive For Relevance

Each post is an opportunity for you to reach your ideal target audience. What questions are they asking? What kind of pain points do they have? By addressing these pain points in question, you're able to reach your target audience at the exact moment they are looking for a solution online.

Stay Focused

Highlight one concept and dive deep into that concept rather than developing multiple, unrelated ideas that are just going to confuse your readers.

Create Intriguing Blog Titles

Optimize for humans first and then do the keyword research necessary to match those queries with the keywords that your ideal audience is typing into Google.

Build Thought Leadership

Thought leadership isn't just about content that's high level. When your content is informative, thought leadership is inevitable.

Post Consistently

Patchy content is the worse. When you blog four times a month you can double your traffic, but when you blog 8 times a month you can triple that traffic.

The marketplace of social networks provides businesses an expansive collection of tools. While it may seem intriguing, it's critical to select the platform that's applicable to your business. Select the platform that identifies with your target audience and share your blog content accordingly. Once you've started to generate a higher volume of website visitors, two things are apparent: The first thing is that it's working and the second thing is that you're now generating more relevant traffic as a result of your content and social efforts.

The problem is that website traffic doesn't pay the bills and it certainly doesn't allow you to close more homes and more remodeling projects.

Convert Your Website Visitors Into Leads

Now we get to the fun part: converting website traffic into qualified leads. A successful lead generation strategy isn't self-serving. It's more about help rather than hype. It's about creating extremely resourceful content that resonates with your ideal clients so much that they just can't wait to call you. This helps warm up your prospects and ensures that you're building a relationship built on trust. Consumers are always looking for resources in their buying journey.

Providing what they need by pushing out helpful content will allow them to take a more organic interest in your company and therefore be more likely to buy from you.

Before you start generating leads, you need to offer something of value in exchange for their coveted contact details. This is called an offer and it's usually in the form of premium content such as a white paper, guide, floor plan, or even a checklist that helps them with their home maintenance chores in the Fall.

Once you create your offer, you need to have a call to action to present that offer on your website. You might be familiar with a call to action. It is simply a graphic with words on your website that guides your website visitors to take the next step with you in some shape or form. At the very least, you probably already have a call to action where you have a schedule a conversation button or form on your website.

However, these calls to action are typically lower in conversions because they require the buyer to be ready for a consultation from you at that moment in time. A higher converting call to action would be a message or a button on your website that gives away immediate value in exchange for contact details, which is the offer that you need to make in order to collect more leads.

Once you create your offer and a call to action in which you can present that offer on your website, you need to direct your website visitors to a place where they can see the offer and read more about it. This is what we call a landing page. A landing page is specifically focused on converting your website visitors into a lead, and a landing page allows you to speak more about your offer as well as provide a form to collect contact information from your website visitors.

Nurture Your Leads Into Clients

At this point you've developed buyer personas that represent your ideal client and you've utilized social media, content creation and search engine optimization to draw more visitors to your site. From there, you've utilized calls to action, landing pages, and forms to convert that traffic to leads.

Are you tired yet? Well pour yourself a cup of coffee because it's now time to show why you've put in so much effort into attracting and converting those leads. Now, it's time to close the deal and convert those leads into a point of sales engagement.

Email lead nurturing is a powerful way to engage with your leads and convert them to a point of sales engagement.

When setting up email workflows you want to have a specific goal in mind. Do you want your leads to ultimately schedule a conversation with you? Whatever that goal is you want to usher your leads down the sales funnel by sending specific emails at specific increments of time. If your leads convert on an email that you sent, your workflows can automatically update your lead's status in the sale cycle. This way you're always up to date on your sales pipeline.

Based on the behaviors and trends of your typical client, you'll want to map out the path that takes the lead down the sales funnel. Here's an example:

When someone downloads your content offer about home renovation tips, your first email will answer a question like, "What are the top tips a homeowner can take to transform their home? The next series of emails would serve to answer the question, "How can the design build process help me transform my home? Then, "Which design build firms can help me?" And finally, "How can I found out more from this company?"

By the end of a successful workflow, your leads have either closed into a contract with your company, or they have gotten to the part of the sales process where your salesperson can now take over.

Delight Your Current Clients Into Raving Fan Promoters

So you've attracted a website visitor, converted that visitor into a lead, nurtured that lead into a qualified sales engagement, and ultimately to a customer. The cycle is complete right? Not so fast.

Once you've successfully attained a client, you need to parlay them into brand advocates of your brand. To do this you need to have happy clients. Monitor and join in on the dialogues that your clients are having on social media channels. If you happen upon a complaint, make a note of it. Make sure that they know you're listening and more importantly, that you understand. You should make your priority to solve for the client, be a solutionist, dig deeper, do your research and unfold the resolution that makes your clients want to refer you to other friends and family in their own networks.

Lastly, measure your ability to delight. To be truly effective, your business must determine how to measure client satisfaction. Start by measuring your net promoter score. Based on a number between 1-10, your net promoter score is the measurement of the percentage of promoters minus the percentage of detractors. If you're turning out a healthy number of promoters, you're on the right track. This is why we delight.

Would you like to access our fast-start marketing bundle for builders and remodelers?

You'll get instant access to cheat sheets and guides that will fast-track you towards running your own marketing engine. Plus receive updates on my best marketing advice and a complimentary consultation offer where we'll map out the exact strategy to help you reach your goals.

Visit www.inboundmill.com/book-bundle

or text your first name and email address to (424) 652-6242

CHAPTER 14
Getting Those Form Fields Filled To The Brim

You can't ask customers what they want and then try to give that to them. By the time you get it built, they'll want something new.

-Steve Jobs

One of the questions I get asked a lot when it comes to getting more leads with a website is, "How do I get people to fill out that form on my website?". The answer to this question is really twofold but I'd to first share a story with you about a client of mine who had a website that wasn't generating leads. What he had was a brochure website; something that was meant to provide some information about his company and his contact details.

What he needed was a lead generating engine.

A lead-generating engine is a website that can easily convert your website visitors into leads. In order to give your website the ability to convert that traffic into qualified leads, you need to have more than just a form for people to fill out just so they could speak with you.

Only 2% of your website traffic is actually going to fill out that contact form on your website. This means that 98% of the people who visit your website are going to click the back button or type in a different URL in the browser. They're going to leave.

Since my client didn't have a contact form on his website, we put up a contact form on his website for starters and began chipping away at finding additional opportunities for the website visitor to provide their contact information in exchange for something valuable that they needed.

The objective was to raise the awareness of a prospective client for the top issues they had questions about, whether it would be about remodeling ideas for their kitchen, bathroom, or just an earnest desire to understand the custom remodeling process.

We have to keep in mind that contact forms on a website come in two flavors.

1. The Low Risk Offer

This is where you're giving away an ebook about kitchen remodeling ideas in exchange for contact details (first name and email address) – that's a lower risk offer. That will lower the friction for a person's decision to give out their contact details because they are not giving a lot of information. Add to the fact that they're getting a lot of immediate value in exchange for that little piece of information and you have a recipe for converting a website visitor into a lead.

2. The High Risk Offer

This is your typical contact form where you ask for a lot of contact details in exchange for a consultation. It's a higher perceived risk to the website visitor because in their minds, they have to dedicate 30-minutes to an hour of their time to speak with a representative at your company. They're giving up their address, phone number and privacy.

Unless they know they can trust you and are ready to do a whole house remodel right now, you're going to have a hard time getting someone to fill out that contact form.

Therefore, by introducing these lower risk offers on my client's website, we were able to triple the amount of qualified leads he was receiving.

Now I just talked about how we overcame the problem of getting more people to fill out that form on the website. We introduced more lower risk offers and thus he was able to convert more website visitors to leads.

However, that's just the tip of the iceberg. We put in a lot of work to come to an understanding of which low risk offers his target clients would want to receive. This type of work is called buyer persona development.

Buyer persona development is all about understanding who your buyers are. It goes deeper than understanding the demographics of your audience, deeper than knowing where they live, deeper than knowing what their income levels are, and deeper than knowing how many members there are in their household.

When you develop your ideal buyer persona, you're understanding how this ideal client actually makes a decision to do business with you. Having access to this type of intel is what will set you apart from your competitors. This type of intel can only be acquired through careful client interviews; interviews with past customers as well as past prospects who didn't end up buying with you.

When you can understand a buyer through the journey that they had to go through in order to arrive at the consideration set of service professionals, then you will understand all of the questions they have and be able to answer those questions with useful content that aligns perfectly at every stage of their decision making process.

To wrap up, it's very important to have a contact form on your website, but you'll need to have a good balance of low risk and high risk offers. Interview your past clients to understand what kind of offers resonate the most with their decision making process.

Would you like to access our fast-start marketing bundle for builders and remodelers?

You'll get instant access to cheat sheets and guides that will fast-track you towards running your own marketing engine. Plus receive updates on my best marketing advice and a complimentary consultation offer where we'll map out the exact strategy to help you reach your goals.

Visit www.inboundmill.com/book-bundle

or text your first name and email address to (424) 652-6242

CHAPTER 15
How To Create Content With ROI In Mind

Don't be afraid to get creative and experiment with your marketing.

-Mike Volpe

Creating content with ROI in mind can be a daunting task.

Knowing what kind of content to create, having the time to create it and knowing what topics resonate with your readers can be really confusing. To tackle this, you must have a process in place.

In our agency, we have a content creation process that doesn't begin until we layout the strategy that facilitates the creation of remarkable content. After laying out the strategy, it ends up as a live document that serves as the blueprint for any content campaign.

How do you come up with a strategy? Easy.

First, identify all of the questions that your prospects are asking online. Seek to understand all of the different questions that your prospects are asking at various stages of the buying process.

The search queries that people type into Google are all prompted by triggers. These triggers are events that cause a person to become aware of a problem. The equity of your home may have increased and now you have the means to move into a better space. This trigger has caused you to search for a solution online with the end goal of wanting to improve the quality of life for you and your loved ones.

When we understand the triggers and the various questions a person would have surrounding the goals they want to meet, we can better help them accomplish their goals at every phase of their decision making process. Once we identify these questions, we can then turn these questions into blog titles, categorize them into topics, and proceed to fill up our editorial calendar.

It is recommended to blog 8 times per month. As a starting point, you should fill your editorial calendar with blog titles and topics for the next 3 months. Then delegate these writing tasks to each of your employees. By writing about a different topic each month, you can measure the performance of your blog posts month over month based on which topic resonates the most with your readers.

By the end of the 90-day period, you'll be able to identify which blog topic performed better than the rest. If topic A in month 1 performed better than topic B and C in month two and three, then chances are you'll want to double down on topic A in the next month going forward. Rinse and repeat and you will have a systemized process of coming up with content to create, distribute and promote.

At the end of every blog post for each topic, you should also have one specific content offer that you can give away in exchange for contact details.

For example, let's say your first month's topic is about a family needing more space. Your blog posts can discuss the custom home process, building a on new lot, and the importance of builder warranties. At the end of each blog post, you might want to give away one premium content offer such as an ebook that goes into detail of how the custom home process works.

By having separate content offers, each being associated with a different topic, you can also measure which topics performed better according to how many content offers were downloaded.

Define the questions your prospects are asking, categorize those questions into topics, and start creating remarkable content!

Would you like to access our fast-start marketing bundle for builders and remodelers?

You'll get instant access to cheat sheets and guides that will fast-track you towards running your own marketing engine. Plus receive updates on my best marketing advice and a complimentary consultation offer where we'll map out the exact strategy to help you reach your goals.

Visit www.inboundmill.com/book-bundle

or text your first name and email address to (424) 652-6242

CHAPTER 16
The Intersection of Consistent Leads and Marketing Automation

The difference between sales and marketing is that marketing owns the message and sales owns the relationship.

-John Jantsch

How do you turn a website visitor into a raving client for your company? Just as you would close a contract when someone walks into a sales office to take a tour of a home, you take them through a similar sales funnel online. A sales funnel has three different stages:

1. Awareness Stage

2. Consideration Stage

3. Decision Stage

A prospect may be in any of these stages by the time they land on your website, so this is an opportunity to provide content that meets them where they are.

Awareness Stage

The awareness stage is at the very top of the funnel where the prospect hasn't had a conversation with sales yet. This person has a lot of questions related to the problems they want or need to solve. To raise their awareness they can either speak directly to sales about these top of mind concerns, do their own research online, or speak with a friend or family member .

An example of a question at the awareness stage is:

- Does my lifestyle fit a closed or open concept kitchen?

You have several content opportunities for establishing trust and thought leadership at the top of the funnel. This can be provided in the following types:

- Photos of different layouts of open concept kitchens

- A blog post about the topic at hand

- Floor plans available for download

- Ebook about open concept kitchen design ideas available for download

Consideration Stage

The next stage is the consideration stage. If the prospect has properly done their due diligence in their research process, this is the stage where the prospect has raised their awareness of the problem at hand and now they are looking to consider which service providers are best suited to solve this problem for them. Some examples of content for the consideration stage are:

- Case study of a whole house remodel

- Ebook about why someone should choose your company as their remodeling firm

- Testimonials from past clients

- Reviews from Houzz

If a prospect has shown interest in your content specific to the consideration stage of their buying journey, then you can provide your brand specific service information and address any pushbacks they would typically have in the sales process. The gloves are off because you've earned their permission to sell them on "why you". These pushbacks can be addressed, for example, in automated follow up emails that go out to a prospect once they have downloaded a case study guide from your website.

Decision Stage

The very last stage is the decision stage. This is the point when a prospect has narrowed down their choices in service providers. They are ready to make a decision to either speak with you or the firm down the street. Enabling a prospect to speak with you doesn't get any simpler than placing a form on your website to schedule a conversation.

Automating The Qualification of Your Leads

Let's put it all together and see how we can qualify the leads that come in through our website without manually keeping track on an excel sheet.

I'll share an example of what this looks like through the work we did to help a remodeling client setup their process.

We first sought to understand the questions that his target clients were asking by identifying a few life events that caused these prospects to establish goals for themselves. In other words, we were predicting common times in a person's life when he or she was going to be in the market for an addition or kitchen remodel. Some of these triggers were either a need for improving the functionality and design features of their existing home or a move-in date was set and they needed the place remodeled before that date.

Once we were able to categorize these triggers, we then proceeded to identify questions they would ask in order to achieve this new goal they set for themselves: Questions like, "Where do I start? How do I define the scope of work? How much should I budget?"

We then answered these questions by developing content offers or ebooks that were given away to prospects in exchange for contact details. Think about this logically: What led you to search on Google or a service provider's website? It was most likely a question you had in your mind. If the service provider had an ebook that answered your question right away, wouldn't you find enough value in that to provide your name and email address? I would guess it would because It takes you a step closer to achieving your remodeling goals.

The ebook offer we developed was, " How To Maximize Your New Remodel Before Moving In". We knew his prospects were interested in understanding how to make the most of their whole house remodel before moving in and when a prospect sees this type of offer on his website, they'll be compelled to download the offer.

When the prospect becomes a lead after downloading this piece of content, they will receive several automated emails that nurture them to a point of sales engagement. These are emails that address several common questions related to that awareness stage offer: Questions like, "How much does the project cost? Why is this approach better than the other? And how long will it take?"

More relevant content is then promoted in each follow up email in an attempt to move the lead to the next stage in the funnel. After a few questions are answered in the emails, the prospect will be much more likely to consume information about his remodeling services. This process of lead nurturing ensures that the lead will identify themselves as someone who is much more interested in considering him as a solution provider without feeling the pressure of a sale.

The kind of content that is promoted in these follow up emails are called consideration stage offers. A consideration stage offer is a critical point in the automated sales process because this offer should be centered around your service and be brand specific. It doesn't just provide helpful information, but also actively sells your brand as a solution to the problem they have.

When a lead takes action on a consideration stage offer that's all about you, you know that they are actively considering your brand as a solution to their problem. This creates a filter in your sales process where leads can now be tagged as marketing qualified and are ready to consume information about your services. Leads at the consideration stage should be treated as if they were looking for more information about your services.

Once the lead decides to download the consideration stage offer such as a case study guide, he'll also be automatically tagged as a marketing qualified lead. Any good CRM should be able to do this automatically for you. Once that lead becomes a marketing qualified lead, he'll then receive another series of emails that seek to close on a consultation, where he'll be offered a consultation that is either on-site or in the office.

This consultation is what we call the decision stage offer. During this time, you're addressing common pushbacks in the emails that are sent to him like, "Why are you more expensive? Why do I have to buy my finishing selections from you?" These pushbacks need to be addressed with answers, again delivered via automated email messages. Typically, testimonials and case studies are promoted via email to marketing qualified leads in order to overcome these pushbacks.

Once the marketing qualified lead takes up your offer to come in your office or book an on-site appointment, the sales conversation has started and you now have the opportunity to close for a contract.

As you can see, you can automate your sales process that models your current process. Utilizing technology and marketing automation, along with a foundational understanding of your buyer personas, you can move leads down a funnel where they are automatically qualified before ever having an actual conversation with you in person or over the phone. This is the engine that will help you qualify your leads and give you a better lead to close.

Would you like to access our fast-start marketing bundle for builders and remodelers?

You'll get instant access to cheat sheets and guides that will fast-track you towards running your own marketing engine. Plus receive updates on my best marketing advice and a complimentary consultation offer where we'll map out the exact strategy to help you reach your goals.

Visit www.inboundmill.com/book-bundle

or text your first name and email address to (424) 652-6242

CHAPTER 17
Leads Are Great, But Qualified Leads Are Even Better

On average, people should be more skeptical when they see numbers. They should be more willing to play around with the data themselves.

-Nate Silver

If you haven't guessed by now, getting better quality leads comes down to one thing: Understanding your buyer personas. Some clients come to me because they want a better qualified client. I can even recall one of my clients saying to me, in his own words, that he was tired of getting "dog sh*t leads". If you're tired of getting just raw leads and want more qualified leads and more of your ideal clients, tell me if any of these statements sound familiar to you.

"People are coming into my showroom and not showing a sense of urgency like the next family who have a move-in date and absolutely need to have their living room remodeled."

"After calling back the person who submitted the contact form on the website, he said to me, 'Oh this wasn't for a free Ipad?' "

"Our referrals don't understand our unique value proposition and we keep spinning our wheels with them."

If you said yes to any of the above, the truth is you need to work on your buyer personas.

Whatever it is that you provide for your clients, your clients all have the same thing: a beating heart. It is your job to differentiate yourself from the pack by letting your clients choose that differentiation. Be careful not to fall into the trap of saying you're different based on how many years in business you've been in. Sure, that's a competitive advantage, but it's not why your clients choose you as their service provider.

You may be in one of two different camps in terms of your backlog of clientele. You're either bursting at the seams of new leads that are all tire kickers and don't value your value proposition or your backlog is just dry. You just need to fill the top of your funnel with fresh leads, so you can close them at a predictable close rate.

Well, the problem with both of these situations is that you're not attracting a qualified lead. What you end up with is a situation where you have an extremely high cost to acquire a new client and a prospect base with numerous pushbacks you can't overcome, which equates to stagnant growth and lack of a backlog filled with qualified leads.

The first step you need to take in developing your buyer personas is understanding your own unique value proposition. We have to first differentiate ourselves to understand who we're targeting.

This reminds me of a story of the architect who had problems differentiating himself. When he was asked what he did for a living, he would just reply, "Well, I design great buildings.". When his customers were asked the same question about what he did, they would respond, "Sure he designs great buildings, but let me tell you what he really does. He gets us past the red tape and helps us get paid faster. That's what he does and that's what we love about him."

This fact has changed the trajectory of his unique value proposition going forward. From then on, this architect regarded himself as the contractor's architect. He was much more focused, and his business essentially skyrocketed from there.

So, how well do you know your differentiation? What is it exactly that you do? Can you name the top 3 decision factors that your ideal buyer uses to select the right builder? Do you understand what triggers your buyer to search for your services? Do you know which X factor to overcome if your buyers are unable to complete the decision to hire you?

Your ideal buyer's journey consists of five rings of insights that serve as the foundation for how you need to be strategically positioned. Buyer personas should tell you what your buyers think about doing business with you. There are two parts to the buyer persona:

1. Your Buyer's Demographics

This is usually readily available through an analyst report and any of your competitors could grab this.

2. Your Buyer's Buying Profile

The actual information you get when you study the buyer within the context of the buying decisions they make. This is how you will beat your competitors and this is often collected through client interviews with past clients and clients you lost

The buying profile contains 5 rings of insights that you must understand. Here are the 5 insights explained:

1. Buyer Initiatives

What happened that caused this buyer to search for a solution like yours? This explains why they invested the time to resolve their pains versus being comfortable with the status quo.

2. Success Factors

What will change in the buyer's circumstances when they choose you? Knowing this helps us build message and content.

3. Perceived Barriers

Why wouldn't the buyer choose your solution? This helps us with decisions for targeting sales enablement and messaging content.

4. Buying Process

What steps will the buyer take to make the decision? This is sometimes called the "buyer's journey" and it must be within the context of the decision we want to influence. Knowing this helps with all marketing decisions, ensuring that you're the company easiest to do business with.

5. Decision Criteria

What aspects of your solution does the buyer weigh to choose you versus your competitors? When we have answers to these questions we're able to prioritize marketing investments and learn why a certain recommended strategy has the highest potential to achieve goals.

With an understanding of the five rings of insight, we have everything we need to produce helpful content on our websites, blog, marketing campaigns, and enable sales to increase their close ratios. And the ROI is this simple: When you know how to make your buyers evaluate your approach on their own terms, you build a bond of trust that competitors can't match. It's the holy grail of all competitive advantages. You have an alignment with sales and marketing and a seamless process of serving your clients with the right proposition at the right time and place.

Buyer persona development is more about the focus on your client and their buying journey and less about what you do as a company. Use it to formulate a strategy that can help you close more qualified leads and clients. Use it to create remarkable content and conversation to position yourself as the clear leader to do business with.

Would you like to access our fast-start marketing bundle for builders and remodelers?

You'll get instant access to cheat sheets and guides that will fast-track you towards running your own marketing engine. Plus receive updates on my best marketing advice and a complimentary consultation offer where we'll map out the exact strategy to help you reach your goals.

Visit www.inboundmill.com/book-bundle

or text your first name and email address to (424) 652-6242

CHAPTER 18
Case Studies: A Closer Look

Design Build Remodeler Boosts Organic Traffic By 4,960%

About Cottage Industries

Cottage Industries is an award-winning, residential design and construction company. Their services include creative architectural design, sound structural engineering, efficient and supportive project management, and fine craftsmanship in all the trades. Their strength is to seamlessly blend old with new, accommodating many architectural styles including Colonial, Victorian, Tudor, Georgian, Contemporary, Farmhouse, Cottage, Splits, and more.

The Problem

The market in Philadelphia is bustling. With new homeowners moving into the city, Cottage Industries knew they had to expand their services into these suburbs in addition to serving the Main Line, a stretch of townships they had been serving for the past 26 years.

With goals of differentiation, increasing leads, and doubling revenue, Cottage Industries began looking for a new marketing strategy and partner who could help reach their goals.

What We Did...

With Inbound Mill's guidance, Cottage Industries began developing their inbound marketing program to generate a consistent stream of qualified leads in their pipeline. Their sales process was mapped out online and new metrics were established to measure the effectiveness of their inbound marketing campaigns.

Using Marketing Automation and Technology To Track And Measure Success

Overall traffic to the website, Twitter and Pinterest followers, new qualified leads, and blog subscribers were new metrics that were tracked using marketing automation software and other technologies. The impact of their inbound marketing program was measured through these metrics to reach their lead generation goals.

By poring over the data points of these important metrics, insights were gleaned about the performance of the content they were creating. Cottage Industries determined whether or not a topic like historic restoration resonated more with their target market than aging in place. This helped them to restructure their future content to improve traffic and conversions, and see if their time and money was bringing them closer to the type of qualified leads they wanted.

Overall, the team wanted to know what marketing efforts were going to bring them the bigger jobs that placed them on the upper-end tier of remodeling projects in their region.

Content Creation

Content was the backbone of their inbound marketing program. Once we established a blueprint of their online sales process, it was time to create content to cater to that process. Content like blog posts and premium content offers such as ebooks were created to drive leads for the company. Prospects were catered to with the right content at the appropriate stages of their buying journey.

Email Marketing & Social Media

After the content was created, Cottage Industries journeyed into the social media landscape. New social media and email campaigns were launched to promote their content in front of prospects who were ready to consume it. Consistent promotions were pushed out on Facebook, Twitter, Pinterest, and Houzz to bring eyeballs back to the hub, their website. Since implementing social media into their inbound marketing program, their **social media traffic increased by 1,480%**

Email campaigns were an integral part of their marketing strategy as they served to delight current clients and consistently engage with prospects with new informational content that helped answer common questions about remodeling. When prospects were ready to move further down the funnel, they were greeted with the appropriate content that helped them understand more about the Cottage Industries brand. Since implementing email campaigns, Cottage Industries has seen a **4,120% increase in traffic from email campaigns.**

Search Engine Optimization

Content marketing requires optimization best practices to make sure that the search engines can index the content being published. Best practices such as including keywords in the meta tags, titles, subheaders, and image alt-tags were followed to make sure Google and Bing were able to read this valuable content. This, in turn, allows prospects to find the helpful content.

When content is properly optimized for the search engines, search rankings are increased. Since optimizing their site, Cottage Industries now has their website on the first page of Google for priority keywords such as kitchen remodeling and bathroom remodeling in their local regions. They have several first page rankings along with multiple listings on those pages. Moreover, their organic search traffic has increased by 4,960%.

Results...

Inbound efforts in the form of blogging, premium content offers, email marketing, and social media marketing combined have helped Cottage Industries **increase their overall website traffic by 203%**. This new increase in traffic has helped them engage with new prospects in a way that is much more personalized, timely, and engaged. It has also helped them achieve one of their major marketing goals- more leads in the pipeline.

Leads in the pipeline are great, but qualified leads are the lifeblood of any business. In order to close more sales, Cottage Industries needed more sales qualified leads who were nurtured and educated about the company's unique value proposition.

Since the redesign and inbound marketing program, Cottage Industries has an **increase of 450% in sales qualified leads in their pipeline**. This has given them more opportunities to have more meaningful conversations to turn into on-site appointments.

Inbound is helping Cottage Industries engage with new prospects and delight their current clients for repeat business. Their content is reaching into new markets in Philadelphia as they improve their brand presence and positioning. This has helped their new prospective clients to understand important aspects of their process such as how optimum value design can help them contain their costs.

More importantly, it has shifted their sales conversations to becoming more of a value add for every project they consult.

Custom Home Builder Sees 740% Increase In Qualified Leads

About Foley Development Group

Foley Development Group, LLC is a custom home builder and remodeler that designs, builds, and remodels homes in Northern Virginia. For 39 years, the company has built a reputation for professionalism, honesty, quality, efficiency, and value with an extensive list of satisfied clients. After 4 decades of quality performance, they have received dozens of awards including several New Home and Renovations 1st place awards nationwide in their respective categories. It's a true testament to their obsession with perfection.

The Problem

Foley Development Group has a long history of building quality homes and performing beautiful remodels for residents in the Northern Virginia area. Over the years, a change in ownership in the family business led to a restructuring of the company's operations. As demand for custom homes grew, the Foley team had to explore new marketing channels to get their message across outside of the tried and true approaches of past client referrals and networking.

The company set out with a goal to transition their product from selling 80% of remodels to building custom homes. This initiative required a fresh stream of qualified new home construction leads and they began searching for a partner who could quickly help them grow their new home construction starts.

What We Did…

Upon starting with Inbound Mill, a website redesign had already been in progress. Instead of starting from scratch, the design team at Inbound Mill restructured the website to focus on the company's new positioning as a custom home builder. In order to make sure that the website was speaking to new home buyers of custom homes, a series of past client interviews were conducted with the company's recent new home construction clients. The purpose was to map out the buyer persona of their ideal client and create messaging and content that resonated at every stage of the buying process. After developing the buyer persona, new website changes were in order: new web copy was written, navigation menu items were added, unnecessary pages were deleted, and a lot of relevant content was produced.

Search Engine Optimization

The new website had to be SEO friendly to the search engines, so that important pages meant to drive traffic from qualified visitors were indexed on the first page of Google. A company blog was created so that each new page of content created was an opportunity to rank for the questions that prospects were asking online. In addition, an influencer outreach campaign was launched to acquire worthy opportunities to guest blog on other sites. Guest blogging helped the company website to acquire authoritative mentions that increased the website's rankings in the search engines.

After just 6 months of working with Inbound Mill, organic traffic now makes up the largest source of traffic for Foley Development Group, with a staggering 11,130% increase in organic traffic.

Email Marketing and Social Media

To keep traffic levels up, more than one channel was utilized. One of the best ways to continually be in front of your new leads is through a blog update email that goes out to your blog subscribers once a week. A cycle of promotion was created by publishing weekly blog posts, distributing it throughout social media and email, and driving visitors back to the website and blog to download new premium content ebook offers. Their most popular ebook is a custom home process guide that informs leads about the custom home building process in Northern Virginia. Since launching email marketing, the Foley team's **email campaigns have led to a boost in traffic by 2,500%**.

The company's social media channels have also become referring sources of qualified leads. They now have accumulated thousands of organic, targeted followers on Pinterest and Twitter alone. They also have new segmented lists of prospects on Facebook who they can run a promotion to at any time to drive new targeted leads. Social media has contributed a 5,900% increase in traffic to the website.

Results...

After working with Inbound Mill for 6 months, Foley Development Group was already seeing tangible results.

Thanks to social media activity, improved search rankings, and strategic email campaigns, Foley Development Group was able to reposition their brand presence and be seen as an authoritative voice in the custom home building industry. As a result, they saw a **740% increase in the number of qualified leads** being generated. The company has already seen a **133% ROI**, however, this was just step one.

To reach Foley Development's biggest goal of increasing their volume of new home construction starts, a search engine optimization push was initiated. To help new custom home prospects find the company, certain priority keywords needed to be ranked on the 1st page of Google. New guest blogging campaigns were launched that promoted infographics and new home construction guides that bloggers loved to write about. Since the push, **Foley Development Group is now on the 1st** page of Google for their priority keywords in the Northern Virginia area as well as Google's 3 pack of local listings.

Overall Foley Development Group has seen the benefits of inbound marketing. They have been able to reach the right audience with the right message at the right time. It's only a matter of time until all of their acquired assets produce consistent dividends in the form of long term leads and clients.

Would you like to access our fast-start marketing bundle for builders and remodelers?

You'll get instant access to cheat sheets and guides that will fast-track you towards running your own marketing engine. Plus receive updates on my best marketing advice and a complimentary consultation offer where we'll map out the exact strategy to help you reach your goals.

Visit www.inboundmill.com/book-bundle

or text your first name and email address to (424) 652-6242

Conclusion

You have to learn the rules of the game. And then you have to play better than anyone else.

-Albert Einstein

I'm going to keep this short and sweet because we're at the end and I just want to give you a heartfelt thanks for giving this book a good read. You now have more context and information to make powerful decisions that will change the trajectory of your business.

Getting inbound leads is a great feeling. The engine that you build to attract leads, the scorecard that you keep to measure your progress, and the systems and platforms you leverage to ensure success all contribute to a healthy business with unbelievable traction.

Please feel free to open up any of the previous chapters to refine what you learned because I'll be the first to admit that it took a while for me to grasp how everything connected together in the digital realm.

Your marketing powers await you. If you need to reach me, you can email me at bobby@inboundmill.com.

www.ingramcontent.com/pod-product-compliance
Lightning Source LLC
Chambersburg PA
CBHW061436180526
45170CB00004B/1435